ORACLE 12C NEW FEATURES
FOR
SQL, PL/SQL & ADMINISTRATION

By
Asim Chowdhury, Technical Architect & Designer

Dedication

This book is dedicated to LORD Krishna and MAA Anandamayee for THE divine blessings

PREFACE

This book is for enthusiast who would like to know 12c new features with real life examples. This book expanded the **following features of 12c SQL:**

- Row limiting clause, expand sqltext of a view, internal parser re-written sql, Invisible column, session level sequence, extended data type, truncate with cascade option, default value for NULL column, auto populate column using sequence and identity type, advanced index compression, Lateral/cross apply/outer apply, multiple index on a column, match_recognise clause for inter-rows pattern, In memory column store etc.

For 12c PL/SQL it has expanded the following features:

- WITH clause improvement, PRAGMA UDF, REDACTION, BEQUEATH clause, Restructuring error stack and backtrace, enhancement in PL/SQL specific data type support in NDS &binding, white listing by means of accessible by clause, Invoker right code using result_cache, improvement in conditional compilation, granting role to stored subprogram instead of user etc.

For 12c ADMINISTRATION it has expanded the following features:

- Adaptive query optimization and online stats gathering, faster online table column addition, DDL LOGGING, adding multiple new partition, global temporary table enhancement, stats gathering improvement, heat map, improvement in auditing using flashback, improvement in tracking security sensitive tables, import & export of version history, free flashback archive and optimize option, Multitenant container database with Pluggable database option etc.

While explaining only 12c new features, I have tried to provide alternative approach prior to 12c also so that the reader can understand the concept with an ease. Hope this 75 pages book will help immensely to learn all the 12c new features and help the reader to use the features in real life confidently. Will appreciate if you can give your feedback in amazon, createspace or any online portal or reach me author.asim@gmail.com

-Author

ACKNOWLEDGEMENT

I would like to thank Stéphane Faroult (author of many Oracle books) who has been guiding me throughout the process. I am inspired by Tom Kyte (man behind asktom.com), Richard Foote (Oracle index specialist), Burleson consulting, Greg Doench (Pearson USA), Steven Feuerstein, I am indebted a lot to them.

My thanks go to Anish Joseph, Nagarjuna Kommineni, Amit Kumar, Abhisek Kumar, Shakti panday, Vishal Jain, Amit Joshi, Amit Chitnis, Avinash Chinchwadkar, Mohsin Hashmi, Venkat, Baskar, Pankaj, Pratap, Deepak, Rashni, Vikash, Swapan, Sumanta and all my colleagues and friends from for their encouraging words. Apologies for not being able to mention the many other names.

My thanks go to my Father Chittaranjan Chowdhury and mother Shephali Chowdhury who taught me how to be simple but think big.

Also my thanks go to my father in-law R.N. Bhui and mother in-law Jharna Bhui for their constant encouragement.

My thanks go to my uncle Ajoy Kar (Professor of Heriot Watt University, Edinburgh) for his encouragement of my work.

My thanks go to my wife Sutapa Chowdhury who inspired me to write this basic book.

My little daughter Aditi is always my inspiration and my thanks go to her for her prayer for the completion of this book. Despite being a small girl she understands the magnitude of the work and inspire me always by her encouraging words. She showed my last 3 books to her school teachers and friends, the smile on her face give me the boost I needed to write the 4th book. She is truly a divine blessing from GOD.

My deep gratitude to Maa Anandamayee and Bashistha maharaja for the divine blessings.

My thanks to Oracle professional and students for accepting my work.

And finally my thanks go to GOD for His constant blessings without which it is impossible to pursue this task.

-Author

Table of Contents:

Chapter 1: ORACLE SQL NEW FEATURE

Data setup
Normal query
Analytical query
Using row limiting clause
Fetch First
OFFSET
WITH Ties
Dbms_utility.expand_sql_text
Parser re-write your query
Invisible column concept
Viewing Invisible column
Moving between Visible to Invisible and vice versa
Invisible column in a view
Finding hidden column
Global and session level sequence
How to create session level sequence
Use of session level sequence
Defining extended data type
Steps to set extended data type
Dynamic memory allocation for VARCHAR2 datatype
Pre-12c to truncate
12c truncate enhancement
ON DELETE CASCADE
ON DELETE SET NULL
Pre-12c issue for default values
12c option to use default value
Pre-12c issue to auto-populate column
12c option to auto-populate column using sequence
IDENTITY TYPE to auto-populate
Compress for OLTP
Advanced Index Compression
Advent of Lateral Clause
Advent of CROSS APPLY Clause
Advent of OUTER APPLY Clause
Solution using correlated subquery
Solution using LATERAL or CROSS APPLY keyword in 12c

Chapter 3: ORACLE ADMINISTRATION NEW FEATURES------------63

8

Chapter 1: ORACLE SQL NEW FEATURE

Feature 1: Top N query using row limiting clause

Here we will explore different ways to get top N rows from a table. In other words we will explore how pagination is done in oracle.

Here is the setup:

```
CREATE TABLE EMP
  (
    EMPLOYEE_ID    NUMBER(4,0),
    EMPLOYEE_NAME VARCHAR2(10 BYTE),
    JOB            VARCHAR2(9 BYTE),
    MANAGER_ID     NUMBER(4,0),
    HIREDATE       DATE,
    SAL         NUMBER(7,2),
    COMMISSION     NUMBER(7,2),
    DEPARTMENT_ID NUMBER(2,0)
  );
```

```
Insert into EMP (EMPLOYEE_ID,EMPLOYEE_NAME,JOB,MANAGER_ID,HIREDATE,SAL,COMMISSION,DEPARTMENT_ID)
values (7369,'SMITH','CLERK',7902,to_date('17-DEC-80','DD-MON-RR'),800,null,20);
Insert into EMP (EMPLOYEE_ID,EMPLOYEE_NAME,JOB,MANAGER_ID,HIREDATE,SAL,COMMISSION,DEPARTMENT_ID)
values (7499,'ALLEN','SALESMAN',7698,to_date('20-FEB-81','DD-MON-RR'),1600,300,30);
Insert into EMP (EMPLOYEE_ID,EMPLOYEE_NAME,JOB,MANAGER_ID,HIREDATE,SAL,COMMISSION,DEPARTMENT_ID)
values (7521,'WARD','SALESMAN',7698,to_date('22-FEB-81','DD-MON-RR'),1250,500,30);
Insert into EMP (EMPLOYEE_ID,EMPLOYEE_NAME,JOB,MANAGER_ID,HIREDATE,SAL,COMMISSION,DEPARTMENT_ID)
values (7566,'JONES','MANAGER',7839,to_date('02-APR-81','DD-MON-RR'),2975,null,20);
Insert into EMP (EMPLOYEE_ID,EMPLOYEE_NAME,JOB,MANAGER_ID,HIREDATE,SAL,COMMISSION,DEPARTMENT_ID)
values (7654,'MARTIN','SALESMAN',7698,to_date('28-SEP-81','DD-MON-RR'),1250,1400,30);
Insert into EMP (EMPLOYEE_ID,EMPLOYEE_NAME,JOB,MANAGER_ID,HIREDATE,SAL,COMMISSION,DEPARTMENT_ID)
values (7698,'BLAKE','MANAGER',7839,to_date('01-MAY-81','DD-MON-RR'),2850,null,30);
Insert into EMP (EMPLOYEE_ID,EMPLOYEE_NAME,JOB,MANAGER_ID,HIREDATE,SAL,COMMISSION,DEPARTMENT_ID)
values (7782,'CLARK','MANAGER',7839,to_date('09-JUN-81','DD-MON-RR'),2450,null,10);
Insert into EMP (EMPLOYEE_ID,EMPLOYEE_NAME,JOB,MANAGER_ID,HIREDATE,SAL,COMMISSION,DEPARTMENT_ID)
values (7788,'SCOTT','ANALYST',7566,to_date('19-APR-87','DD-MON-RR'),3000,null,20);
Insert into EMP (EMPLOYEE_ID,EMPLOYEE_NAME,JOB,MANAGER_ID,HIREDATE,SAL,COMMISSION,DEPARTMENT_ID)
values (7839,'KING','PRESIDENT',null,to_date('17-NOV-81','DD-MON-RR'),5000,null,10);
Insert into EMP (EMPLOYEE_ID,EMPLOYEE_NAME,JOB,MANAGER_ID,HIREDATE,SAL,COMMISSION,DEPARTMENT_ID)
values (7844,'TURNER','SALESMAN',7698,to_date('08-SEP-81','DD-MON-RR'),1500,0,30);
Insert into EMP (EMPLOYEE_ID,EMPLOYEE_NAME,JOB,MANAGER_ID,HIREDATE,SAL,COMMISSION,DEPARTMENT_ID)
values (7876,'ADAMS','CLERK',7788,to_date('23-MAY-87','DD-MON-RR'),1100,null,20);
Insert into EMP (EMPLOYEE_ID,EMPLOYEE_NAME,JOB,MANAGER_ID,HIREDATE,SAL,COMMISSION,DEPARTMENT_ID)
values (7900,'JAMES','CLERK',7698,to_date('03-DEC-81','DD-MON-RR'),950,null,30);
Insert into EMP (EMPLOYEE_ID,EMPLOYEE_NAME,JOB,MANAGER_ID,HIREDATE,SAL,COMMISSION,DEPARTMENT_ID)
values (7902,'FORD','ANALYST',7566,to_date('03-DEC-81','DD-MON-RR'),3000,null,20);
Insert into EMP (EMPLOYEE_ID,EMPLOYEE_NAME,JOB,MANAGER_ID,HIREDATE,SAL,COMMISSION,DEPARTMENT_ID)
values (7934,'MILLER','CLERK',7782,to_date('23-JAN-82','DD-MON-RR'),1300,null,10);
COMMIT;
```

Prior to Oracle 12c, to get the top ten salaries of EMP table the following queries were used:

Normal query:

```
SELECT * FROM
  ( SELECT * FROM emp ORDER BY sal DESC
  ) WHERE rownum<11;
```

Analytical query:

```
select * from
(
select a.*,row_number() over (order by sal desc) rn from emp a
)
where rn=1;
```

Basic Syntax for TOP N query using ROW limiting clause in 12c:

```
[ OFFSET offset { ROW | ROWS } ]
[ FETCH { FIRST | NEXT } [ { rowcount | percent PERCENT } ]
    { ROW | ROWS } { ONLY | WITH TIES } ]
```

So to get top 10 rows just run:

```
SELECT * FROM emp ORDER BY SAL DESC
FETCH FIRST 10 ROWS ONLY;
```

EMPLOYEE_ID	EMPLOYEE_NAME	JOB	MANAGER_ID	HIREDATE	SAL	COMMISSION	DEPARTMENT_ID
7839	KING	PRESIDENT	(null)	17-NOV-81	5000	(null)	10
7788	SCOTT	ANALYST	7566	19-APR-87	3000	(null)	20
7902	FORD	ANALYST	7566	03-DEC-81	3000	(null)	20
7566	JONES	MANAGER	7839	02-APR-81	2975	(null)	20
7698	BLAKE	MANAGER	7839	01-MAY-81	2850	(null)	30
7782	CLARK	MANAGER	7839	09-JUN-81	2450	(null)	10
7499	ALLEN	SALESMAN	7698	20-FEB-81	1600	300	30
7844	TURNER	SALESMAN	7698	08-SEP-81	1500	0	30
7934	MILLER	CLERK	7782	23-JAN-82	1300	(null)	10
7521	WARD	SALESMAN	7698	22-FEB-81	1250	500	30

If there are duplicate SAL values then you can still receive them using "WITH TIES" clause. WITH TIES clause will return more rows if Nth rows value is duplicate. For this case 10th rows SAL is 1250 and this is duplicate and hence return more rows:

```
SELECT * FROM emp ORDER BY SAL DESC
FETCH FIRST 10 rows
WITH TIES;
```

EMPLOYEE_ID	EMPLOYEE_NAME	JOB	MANAGER_ID	HIREDATE	SAL	COMMISSION	DEPARTMENT_ID
7839	KING	PRESIDENT	(null)	17-NOV-81	5000	(null)	10
7788	SCOTT	ANALYST	7566	19-APR-87	3000	(null)	20
7902	FORD	ANALYST	7566	03-DEC-81	3000	(null)	20
7566	JONES	MANAGER	7839	02-APR-81	2975	(null)	20
7698	BLAKE	MANAGER	7839	01-MAY-81	2850	(null)	30
7782	CLARK	MANAGER	7839	09-JUN-81	2450	(null)	10
7499	ALLEN	SALESMAN	7698	20-FEB-81	1600	300	30
7844	TURNER	SALESMAN	7698	08-SEP-81	1500	0	30
7934	MILLER	CLERK	7782	23-JAN-82	1300	(null)	10
7521	WARD	SALESMAN	7698	22-FEB-81	1250	500	30
7654	MARTIN	SALESMAN	7698	28-SEP-81	1250	1400	30

In order to get top 10% of salary records from EMP table:

```
SELECT * FROM emp ORDER BY SAL DESC
FETCH FIRST 10 PERCENT ROWS ONLY;
```

In order to get 6th to 10th records from top 10 salaried records:
```
SELECT * FROM emp ORDER BY SAL DESC OFFSET 5 ROWS
FETCH NEXT 5 ROWS ONLY;
```

OFFSET 5 means skip first 5 records.
The output:

EMPLOYEE_ID	EMPLOYEE_NAME	JOB	MANAGER_ID	HIREDATE	SAL	COMMISSION	DEPARTMENT_ID
7782	CLARK	MANAGER	7839	09-JUN-81	2450	(null)	10
7499	ALLEN	SALESMAN	7698	20-FEB-81	1600	300	30
7844	TURNER	SALESMAN	7698	08-SEP-81	1500	0	30
7934	MILLER	CLERK	7782	23-JAN-82	1300	(null)	10
7521	WARD	SALESMAN	7698	22-FEB-81	1250	500	30

Note: All the above SQL can be directly used in PL/SQL
E.g.
```
DECLARE
   Type t_sal IS TABLE OF emp.sal%type INDEX BY BINARY INTEGER;
   v_sal t_sal;
BEGIN
   SELECT sal bulk collect INTO v_sal FROM emp ORDER BY sal DESC OFFSET 5 ROWS
   FETCH NEXT 5 ROWS only;
END;
/
```
However in this example if you use bind variable (i.e. in DECLARE section add bind_nr number :=5; and in BEGIN section instead of "5 ROWS" use "bind_nr ROWS") , it will fail with error because of oracle bug in 12c (Bug is related with datatype), when used in "OFFSET/FETCH NEXT" clause. The possible workaround is as below:
Use to_number(bind_nr) ROWS instead of bind_nr ROWS [5 ROWS] in the above PL/SQL block.

Feature 2: Recursively expand sqltext of a view and find how parser rewrite the SQL

Ever struggled to get the definition of recursive views? Here we will discuss how to view full text for all the recursive views and also find the re-written SQL by oracle parser.

A view is used to hide the complexity of code from the developer and also to reduce redundant code in an application as 1 view can be referred to by multiple other views. Prior to oracle 12c to debug any issue you need to expand the sql of all the dependent views of the main view and analyse. This is very tedious exercise especially when recursive depth is large. Good news, Oracle 12c R1 provides the facility to expand the sql text to see the full SQL reference of the view with full reference of dependent recursive views.

Here is very simple dummy example to demonstrate how it works:

```
CREATE TABLE t1
  (owner VARCHAR2(10),object_name VARCHAR2(30),created DATE
  );
CREATE OR REPLACE VIEW v1
AS
  SELECT owner,object_name,created FROM t1;

CREATE OR REPLACE VIEW v2
AS
  SELECT * FROM v1 WHERE created BETWEEN sysdate-5 AND sysdate;

CREATE OR REPLACE VIEW v3
AS
  SELECT * FROM v2 WHERE object_name LIKE 'TEST%';
```

Now to expand v3 we use dbms_utility.expand_sql_text as below:

Make sure you give grant execute on dbms_utility to your user.

```
SET SERVEROUTPUT ON
DECLARE
  v_output CLOB;
BEGIN
  DBMS_UTILITY.expand_sql_text ( input_sql_text => 'SELECT * FROM v3',
                                 output_sql_text => v_output );
  DBMS_OUTPUT.put_line(v_output);
END;
/
```

The output will look like:

```
SELECT "A1"."OWNER" "OWNER","A1"."OBJECT_NAME" "OBJECT_NAME","A1"."CREATED" "CREATED" FROM
(SELECT "A2"."OWNER" "OWNER","A2"."OBJECT_NAME" "OBJECT_NAME","A2"."CREATED" "CREATED" FROM
(SELECT "A3"."OWNER" "OWNER","A3"."OBJECT_NAME" "OBJECT_NAME","A3"."CREATED" "CREATED" FROM
(SELECT "A4"."OWNER" "OWNER","A4"."OBJECT_NAME" "OBJECT_NAME","A4"."CREATED" "CREATED" FROM SYS."T1" "A4") "A3"
WHERE "A3"."CREATED">=SYSDATE-5 AND "A3"."CREATED"<=SYSDATE) "A2" WHERE "A2"."OBJECT_NAME" LIKE 'TEST%') "A1"
```

Note **DBMS_UTILITY.expand_sql_text** not only replaces recursively all the views referred in the input SQL query but it also provides how oracle parser rewrite the code while doing the expansion of SQL.
E.g.
As provided in this Chapter 3: Feature 1: Top N query using row limiting clause

Let us take the same example to show how oracle rewrite the code internally:

```
SELECT * FROM emp ORDER BY SAL DESC
FETCH NEXT 5 ROWS ONLY;
```

You pass this SQL statement to the **expand_sql_text** as below:

```
SET serveroutput ON
DECLARE
  v_output CLOB;
BEGIN
  DBMS_UTILITY.expand_sql_text( input_sql_text => 'select * from emp order by sal desc fetch next 5 rows only', output_sql_text=>v_output);
  DBMS_OUTPUT.put_line(v_output);
END;
/
```

The <u>output</u> will expand the SQL and shown below how your SQL has been rewritten by oracle parser:

```
SELECT "A1"."EMPLOYEE_ID" "EMPLOYEE_ID",
  "A1"."EMPLOYEE_NAME" "EMPLOYEE_NAME",
  "A1"."JOB" "JOB",
  "A1"."MANAGER_ID" "MANAGER_ID",
  "A1"."HIREDATE" "HIREDATE",
  "A1"."SAL" "SAL",
  "A1"."COMMISSION" "COMMISSION",
  "A1"."DEPARTMENT_ID" "DEPARTMENT_ID"
FROM
  (SELECT "A2"."EMPLOYEE_ID" "EMPLOYEE_ID",
    "A2"."EMPLOYEE_NAME" "EMPLOYEE_NAME",
    "A2"."JOB" "JOB",
    "A2"."MANAGER_ID" "MANAGER_ID",
    "A2"."HIREDATE" "HIREDATE",
    "A2"."SAL" "SAL",
    "A2"."COMMISSION" "COMMISSION",
    "A2"."DEPARTMENT_ID" "DEPARTMENT_ID",
    "A2"."SAL" "rowlimit_$_0",
    ROW_NUMBER() OVER ( ORDER BY "A2"."SAL" DESC ) "rowlimit_$$_rownumber"
  FROM "EMP" "A2"
  ) "A1"
WHERE "A1"."rowlimit_$$_rownumber"<=5
ORDER BY "A1"."rowlimit_$_0" DESC;
```

Feature 3: Invisible column

Here we will discuss how to make a column invisible to all and visible to those who are aware of the existence of the column.

<u>Invisible index</u> and <u>virtual column</u> were introduced in oracle 11gR1 and **Invisible column** was introduced in Oracle 12c. **Invisible column** concept came from the requirement of data hiding which used to be done using Oracle view or some kind of security filter using FGAC.

In Oracle 12c R1 you can have an <u>invisible column</u> in a table. So once you define a column as invisible that column will not appear in generic query (i.e. SELECT * FROM ...).
You **can see the column**
- By explicitly referring to the column name in "**select**" or "**insert**" statement

13

- By describing the table (provided you use SET command in sql*plus in 12c
  SET COLINVISIBLE ON|OFF)

Any normal column, **virtual column** and partition column can be defined as **invisible**
However external table, temporary table and cluster table will not support invisible column.

Here is the syntax to create invisible column
```
CREATE TABLE emp
 (empno NUMBER,
 ename VARCHAR2(40),
 sal NUMBER(9,4) INVISIBLE
 );
```

In order to convert a column from invisible to visible use:
```
ALTER TABLE emp MODIFY (sal VISIBLE );
```

In order to convert a column from visible to invisible again use:
```
ALTER TABLE emp MODIFY (sal INVISIBLE );
```

Finding hidden column:
You can find the list of invisible columns using:
```
SELECT owner,table_name,column_name,hidden_column
FROM all_tab_cols
WHERE owner    = 'U1'
AND table_name = 'EMP';
```

Notes:
> In 12c, **even in a view** you can make a column invisible:
```
CREATE OR REPLACE VIEW emp_vw (empno, ename, sal INVISIBLE)
AS
    SELECT empno, ename, sal FROM emp;
```

> In 12c you can make a **virtual column** also visible and invisible similar to a normal column.

> Invisible columns are not considered when you use TABLE_NAME%ROWTYPE

Feature 4: Session level sequence

Here we will discuss how to reset a sequence value for any new session automatically.

In oracle 12c you can create session level sequence by using keyword "session". The default one is global. Session level sequence produces unique values for a session and once the session ends the sequence is reset, unlike global level session.
Session sequence performs better than global sequence because session sequence does not keep anything in data dictionary. However session sequence can be used only in a few specific scenarios

- During loading to staging table where the sequence is used by single session.
- As a surrogate key in global temporary table

The syntax for creating and converting to session and global level is given below:

```
CREATE SEQUENCE session_seq START WITH 1 INCREMENT BY 1 SESSION;

ALTER SEQUENCE session_seq GLOBAL|SESSION;
```

Feature 5: Extended data type & parametrization of variable length

Here we will discuss how in 12c database table the size of VARCHAR2 can be of size 32767 byte as against 4000 byte in 11gR2.

Prior to Oracle 12c maximum size of RAW, VARCHAR2, NVARCHAR2 data type table columns were 2000, 4000 and 4000 respectively.
In oracle 12c the size of these data types has been extended up to 32767 bytes in database table column.
In order to use the extended character size in 12c you need to set the initialization parameter **MAX_STRING_SIZE** to EXTENDED. The default value is STANDARD. If default value STANDARD is used then the size of these column will be same as it was prior to 12c.

Steps to set the parameter:

```
SHUTDOWN;
STARTUP UPGRADE;
ALTER system SET max_string_size = EXTENDED scope=spfile;
Run $ORACLE_HOME/rdbms/admin/utl32k.sql
SHUTDOWN IMMEDIATE;
STARTUP;
```

Once you upgrade your database to use setting EXTENDED you cannot revert it to STANDARD.

Advantage of using extended data types is that it will reduce the requirement to use LOB data types most of the time.

Note: From 11g onward PGA memory allocation is dynamic if you declare a VARCHAR2 variable of size greater than 4000. If you declare a variable less than or equal to 4000 byte then PGA memory is fully allocated (i.e. not dynamic). And hence it is suggested to declare a variable to a size greater than 4000 in case you are not sure of approx. length of the variable. By declaring the VARCHAR2 bigger you save large amount of PGA memory.

Parametrization of variable length: From Oracle 12.2 onward we can parametrize the size of a varchar2 variable. So instead of b VARCHAR2 (10) you can use b VARCHAR2 (package constant) as shown below:

```
CREATE OR REPLACE PACKAGE pck
IS  a CONSTANT NUMBER :=10;
END pck;
/
DECLARE
  b VARCHAR2(pck.a);
BEGIN
  NULL;
END;
/
```

Feature 6: Truncate table cascade

Here we will discuss how to truncate a parent table which has a relation with child table.

Prior to oracle 12c if any table is referred to by a child table using foreign key relationship then you cannot truncate the parent table.
Even if there is no data present in child table, still the truncate option will not work for parent table, it will give an error:

```
TRUNCATE table P1

SQL Error: ORA-02266: unique/primary keys in table referenced by enabled foreign
02266. 00000 -  "unique/primary keys in table referenced by enabled foreign keys
*Cause:      An attempt was made to truncate a table with unique or
             primary keys referenced by foreign keys enabled in another table.
             Other operations not allowed are dropping/truncating a partition of a
             partitioned table or an ALTER TABLE EXCHANGE PARTITION.
*Action:     Before performing the above operations the table, disable the
             foreign key constraints in other tables. You can see what
             constraints are referencing a table by issuing the following
             command:
             SELECT * FROM USER_CONSTRAINTS WHERE TABLE_NAME = "tabnam";
```

So prior to oracle 12c you have <u>two **options** </u>**(As you cannot use truncate when you have child table)**

➤ Delete all the dependencies and then delete the parent table:
   E.g.

   In the above scenario in order to delete "P1" table you need to traverse the tree and find out all the dependencies and then you need to delete in the following sequence only
   gc1->gc2->c1->c2>P1
   I have shown only 2 levels however the dependency tree can go to any level and there may be interdependency between child tables. So it can be very tricky to find all the recursive dependencies and execute the delete.

➤ Foreign key is implemented using below command by default:
```
ALTER TABLE C1 ADD CONSTRAINT EMP_FK1 FOREIGN KEY (dept_id)
REFERENCES P1(dept_id);
```
   And hence if you fire
```
DELETE FROM P1;
```

   It will fail with error
```
02292. 00000 - "integrity constraint (%s.%s) violated - child record found"
```
   So the solution is:
   Recreate the foreign key constraint with "ON DELETE CASCADE"
```
ALTER TABLE C1 ADD CONSTRAINT EMP_FK1 FOREIGN KEY (dept_id)
REFERENCES P1(dept_id) ON DELETE CASCADE;
```

   And then fire:

```
DELETE FROM P1;
```
This will delete records from child tables too.

However in <u>Oracle 12c</u> you can use Truncate as below:
```
TRUNCATE table P1 CASCADE
```

This will automatically initiate recursive truncate of all the child tables and then the parent table.
However note for this option to work you must have foreign key present in all the child tables with reference as ON DELETE CASCADE using the command as below (here "emp" is child table and "DEPT" is parent table)
```
ALTER TABLE C1 ADD CONSTRAINT EMP_FK1 FOREIGN KEY (dept_id)
REFERENCES P1(dept_id) ON DELETE CASCADE;
```

Note: since "ON DELETE CASCADE" silently, without any warning, deletes rows from child tables it is sometime a business requirement <u>not to delete the child rows</u> and instead update the child rows setting parent column **value to null**. In order to do that use below step:
```
ALTER TABLE C1 DROP CONSTRAINT EMP_FK1;

ALTER TABLE C1 ADD CONSTRAINT EMP_FK1 FOREIGN KEY (dept_id)
REFERENCES P1(dept_id) ON DELETE SET NULL;
```

So this will not remove rows from child tables, rather it will just update the reference parent column to null in the child tables.

Feature 7: Create default value for NULL column

Here we will explore how to use a default value even if you mistakenly insert null for a table column.

Prior to Oracle 12c when you want to keep a default value for the nullable column you use DEFAULT keyword in table creation. <u>However when you insert null the default value is lost.</u>
```
CREATE TABLE t
  (a NUMBER PRIMARY KEY,
  b NUMBER DEFAULT 12
  );

INSERT INTO t(a) VALUES(1);
INSERT INTO t(a,b) VALUES(2,NULL);
INSERT INTO t(a,b) VALUES(3,23);
COMMIT;
```

Now when you run a select you will see
```
SELECT * FROM t;
```

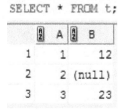

	A	B
1	1	12
2	2	(null)
3	3	23

Note in 1st insert statement we have omitted the default column and hence it takes the default column value 12 for A=1
In 3rd Insert statement I have explicitly mentioned column value 23 for column "b" and hence it has taken that value 23 for A=3

17

<u>Now the problem is in 2nd insert. When we insert null in column "b" the default value 12 is ignored.</u>

In order to resolve this before Oracle 12c you have to have logic in your application to check if the value is null then set it to default.

However in Oracle 12c you need not do this, it will automatically use the default value if you insert NULL in that column. This is possible because of the construct "DEFAULT ON NULL"

```
CREATE TABLE t
  (a NUMBER PRIMARY KEY,
   b NUMBER DEFAULT ON NULL 12
  );

INSERT INTO t(a) VALUES(1);
INSERT INTO t(a,b) VALUES(2,NULL);
INSERT INTO t(a,b) VALUES(3,23);
COMMIT;
```

Now when you run a select you will see

```
SELECT * FROM t;
```

	A		B
1	1		12
2	2		12
3	3		23

<u>Note:</u> **If the table** "t" is created with "b number default 12" (instead of "b number default ON NULL 12" introduced in 12c) then if you insert "NULL" then it will store "NULL". If you do not insert anything in the column "b" then it will use the default value "12".

Feature 8: Auto-populate column using Sequence as Column default value

Here we will discuss mechanism to auto populate primary key column using sequence without the use of trigger.

Prior to Oracle 12c you cannot use sequence_name.nextval to create a default column value. In order to do that you need to make use of a trigger as below:

```
CREATE SEQUENCE t_seq START WITH 1;
DROP TABLE t;
CREATE TABLE t
  (a NUMBER PRIMARY KEY,
   b NUMBER DEFAULT 12
  );
CREATE OR REPLACE TRIGGER t_trig BEFORE INSERT ON t FOR EACH ROW
BEGIN
  IF :new.a IS NULL THEN :new.a :=t_seq.nextval;
END IF;
END t_trig;
/
```

Now if you run

```
INSERT INTO t(b) VALUES(24);
```

Table "t" will have a record as below where column A has been populated by the trigger:

A	B
1	1	24

In Oracle 12c you need not use a trigger as you can directly use **nextval** attribute of sequence to create default column value as shown below:

```
CREATE SEQUENCE t_seq START WITH 1;
DROP TABLE t;
CREATE TABLE t
  (a NUMBER DEFAULT t_seq.nextval PRIMARY KEY,
   b NUMBER DEFAULT ON NULL 12
  );
```

Now if you insert a record it will populate the primary key "a" from the sequence t_seq

```
SET serveroutput ON
DECLARE
  var_a NUMBER;
BEGIN
  INSERT INTO t(b) VALUES(17) RETURNING a INTO var_a;
  dbms_output.put_line('value is:'||var_a);
END;
/
```

Output:

```
PL/SQL procedure successfully completed.

value is:1
```

Note: Throughput of application improve dramatically when you use sequence.nextval instead of trigger based approach to populate a default column in 12c.

Feature 9: Default primary key column value using IDENTITY type

Here we will discuss mechanism to auto populate primary key column using IDENTITY type in 12c without the use of trigger.

Prior to Oracle 12c if you want to default the primary key column value you need to take the help of trigger as shown in the above Feature 8,
In Oracle 12c you can default the primary key column value using .NEXTVAL attribute of sequence as shown in the above Feature 9.
Alternatively in 12c you can use IDENTITY type for the same purpose. So without using a sequence you can populate the primary key with default value as shown below:

```
CREATE TABLE t
  (
    a NUMBER GENERATED AS IDENTITY PRIMARY KEY,
    b NUMBER DEFAULT ON NULL 12
  );
```
You can set the default column value and choose the next number
```
CREATE TABLE t
  (
    a NUMBER GENERATED BY DEFAULT AS IDENTITY (
    START WITH 10 INCREMENT BY 2) PRIMARY KEY,
    b NUMBER DEFAULT ON NULL 12
  );
```

Basically Identity type will internally create a sequence similar to a database sequence and assign that value to the default primary key column.

Feature 10: Get approx. distinct count of rows

Oracle 12c has introduced function **Approx_count_distinct** (column_name).

This will give **approximate** total number of **distinct, NOT NULL values** of column_name in a table. Performance improvement using this function is significant as compared to **Count** (distinct column name) and hence when you do not have requirement to display the exact distinct count then you can make use of this function for any of your reporting requirements.

Feature 11: Table compression/Index compression in 12c

Here we will look into saving space in database and improving performance by compression of table/index and also we will look into oracle 12c Advanced Index compression while rebuilding or creating an index.

Compression was introduced in Oracle 8i where you can compress only index keys. Oracle 9i added compression for Tables but it can only be done while creating via direct load or CTAS or Insert with Append. Oracle 11g introduced advanced compression where you can create a table with **COMPRESS FOR OLTP**.
```
CREATE TABLE tabl
  (
    a NUMBER,
    b VARCHAR2 (30),
    c VARCHAR2 (20)
  )
  COMPRESS FOR OLTP;
```
Also you can compress a table after creation using Alter command.
```
ALTER TABLE tabl move COMPRESS;
```

Run the following query **before** the alter command and **after** the ALTER command to see how much space is regained by compression. Compression not only saves space but any query against the table after compression has <u>improved performance</u> as the number of BLOCKs scanned is reduced dramatically.

```
SELECT segment_name,
  segment_type,
  blocks
FROM dba_segments
WHERE segment_name IN ('TAB1');
```

Similarly while creating or rebuilding index you can use compression which allows us to store the index in fewer database blocks which not only save space but improve performance on large index range scan and index fast full scan.

```
ALTER INDEX index_name REBUILD ONLINE COMPRESS;
```

However one <u>must be careful</u> before compressing a particular index. If an index does not have lot of repeated data compression of index may <u>lead to increase in storage space</u> because of oracle internal mechanism of storing the index blocks.

You can see amount of space occupied by index (which can be run <u>before</u> and <u>after</u> compression):

```
SELECT index_name,
  leaf_blocks,--This will provide the storage space of index
  compression
FROM user_indexes
WHERE table_name='TABLE_NAME';
```

However from **Oracle 12c** onwards you need not worry whether compression will lead to increase in storage space because oracle 12c has introduced "**Advanced Index compression**" which will always decrease the storage space and improve performance for index range scan. This advanced feature is available only in enterprise edition.

In order to use "**Advanced Index compression**" just use the keyword "compress advanced low" while creating/rebuilding the index.

```
ALTER INDEX index_name REBUILD COMPRESS ADVANCED LOW;
```

After compressing an index using this option you can run the above "SELECT" query and will see that the leaf_blocks value is significantly lesser.

Note: "Advanced Index compression" does not work on <u>unique single-column indexes</u>.

Feature 12: LATERAL/CROSS APPLY and OUTER APPLY

Here we are going to discuss **Oracle 12c** new construct "**LATERAL/CROSS APPLY**" and **OUTER APPLY**

<u>**Objective:**</u> To get max sal in a department and corresponding ename and dept_id

<u>Solution using correlated subquery:</u>

```
SELECT ename,dept_id,sal
FROM emp a
WHERE sal=
  (SELECT MAX(sal) FROM emp b WHERE a.dept_id=b.dept_id
  );
```

Here in the subquery, inner table "**EMP b**" joins with outer table "**EMP a**".

<u>Solution using LATERAL or CROSS APPLY keyword in 12c:</u>

21

Oracle 12c has introduced LATERAL syntax to correlate inline views. In other words using LATERAL/CROSS APPLY keyword let you reference an item similar to normal join.

The above correlated subquery can be re-written using LATERAL keyword:

```
SELECT a.*,x.ename
FROM  (SELECT MAX(sal) salary,dept_id FROM emp GROUP BY dept_id)a,
LATERAL
(SELECT sal,dept_id,ename FROM emp b WHERE a.dept_id=b.dept_id AND b.sal=a.salary
)x;
```

Note you are able to refer to "**table alias a**" within an "**inline view x**" by virtue of LATERAL keyword.
Using CROSS APPLY the syntax is:

```
SELECT a.*,x.ename
FROM  (SELECT MAX(sal) salary,dept_id FROM emp GROUP BY dept_id)a
CROSS APPLY
(SELECT sal,dept_id,ename FROM emp b WHERE a.dept_id=b.dept_id AND b.sal=a.salary
)x;
```

Note: "**,**" before the LATERAL keyword is removed when you use CROSS APPLY. Both LATERAL and CROSS APPLY work **like normal INNER JOIN**

Solution using inline view:

If you do not use the "LATERAL" keyword then you can not refer other table inside an inline view "alias x" you have to join the inline view with other table seperately as below:

```
SELECT a.*,x.ename
FROM  (SELECT MAX(sal) salary,dept_id FROM emp GROUP BY dept_id)a,
(SELECT sal,dept_id,ename FROM emp b)x
where
a.dept_id=x.dept_id AND a.salary=x.sal
```

Solution using normal subquery:
```
SELECT ename,dept_id,sal
FROM emp
WHERE (dept_id,sal) IN
  (SELECT dept_id,MAX(sal) FROM emp GROUP BY dept_id
  );
```

Regrding the use of "LATERAL" keyword let us take one more example:

```
CREATE TABLE task_t(task_name VARCHAR2(10),no_of_activity NUMBER
  );
INSERT INTO task_t VALUES('Task 1',5);
INSERT INTO task_t VALUES('Task 2',3);
INSERT INTO task_t VALUES('Task 3',4);
INSERT INTO task_t VALUES('Task 4',6);
INSERT INTO task_t VALUES('Task 5',2);
```

Now the requirement is to construct and display activity name based on number of activity against each task name. So if "no_of_activity" is 5 for a task then you need to construct 5 activities.

Here is the **solution** using LATERAL clause in 12c:

```
SELECT t.task_name,t.no_of_activity,act_break.activity_name
FROM task_t t,
LATERAL
(SELECT 'activity '||rownum AS activity_name FROM dual CONNECT BY rownum<t.no_of_activity+1) act_break
ORDER BY t.task_name,
   act_break.activity_name;
```

The output look as below:

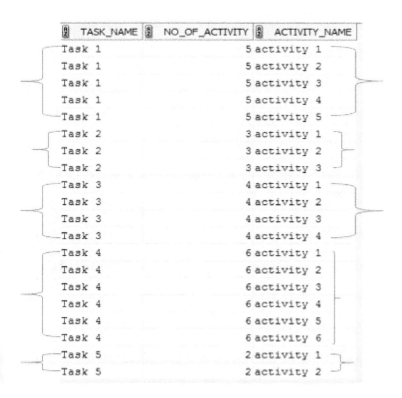

TASK_NAME	NO_OF_ACTIVITY	ACTIVITY_NAME
Task 1	5	activity 1
Task 1	5	activity 2
Task 1	5	activity 3
Task 1	5	activity 4
Task 1	5	activity 5
Task 2	3	activity 1
Task 2	3	activity 2
Task 2	3	activity 3
Task 3	4	activity 1
Task 3	4	activity 2
Task 3	4	activity 3
Task 3	4	activity 4
Task 4	6	activity 1
Task 4	6	activity 2
Task 4	6	activity 3
Task 4	6	activity 4
Task 4	6	activity 5
Task 4	6	activity 6
Task 5	2	activity 1
Task 5	2	activity 2

The above query will fail without the LATERAL keyword with error:
ORA-00904: "T"."NO_OF_ACTIVITY": invalid identifier

So without LATERAL clause it will be little tricky to derive the solution as shown in following example:

```
SELECT t.task_name,t.no_of_activity,act_break.activity_name
FROM task_t t,
   (SELECT rownum AS rn,'activity '||rownum AS activity_name FROM dual CONNECT BY rownum<10)act_break
WHERE rn<t.no_of_activity+1
ORDER BY t.task_name,
   act_break.activity_name;
```

This is simple example however when you have some complex query where you need to derive rowset based on other table in the "FROM" clause then it will be tricky to write code without "LATERAL" keyword.

So as you can see "LATERAL" keyword is very powerful in terms of ease of use as you just need to place "LATERAL" keyword between two tables/inline views. In the inline view you are able to refer to other tables as you do in corelated subquery.

OUTER APPLY in 12c:

This works like LEFT OUTER JOIN and hence returns all the rows from LEFT table. The advantage of this construct is similar to LATERAL/CROSS APPLY i.e from INLINE VIEW you can refer a table on the LEFT of the INLINE VIEW (similar to correlated subquery).

For example just REPLACE as below from the above examples:
",LATERAL" by "OUTER APPLY"
"CROSS APPLY" by "OUTER APPLY"

Feature 13: Multiple indexes on same column

Here we will understand how to reduce database downtime and avoid subsequent issues (whilst a new type of index is created after old index is dropped) by maintaining different kinds of index on the same column.

Having **multiple indexes** on same set of columns allows you to switch between indexes based on situation and application requirement and also lets you quickly see the impact of various types of index on the same set of columns in the application. Multiple indexes will be useful when you want to convert from one type of index to other type of index with a minimal downtime. **However only one of the indexes on the column will be visible at single point of time.**

Also note we can create more than 1 index on 1 column or set of columns only if index type **is different and one of the index is visible at single point of time**.

Pre **12c** we could never create more than 1 index on 1 column or set of columns. In **12c only** we can do that.

Note in Oracle 11gR1 **invisible index** was introduced. Now we have to use the invisible index concept to create multiple indexes on same column.

E.g.
```
CREATE TABLE EMP(EMPNO NUMBER,ENAME VARCHAR2(30),SAL NUMBER,HIRE_DATE DATE);
INSERT INTO EMP VALUES(1,'STEVE',2546,SYSDATE-100);
INSERT INTO EMP VALUES(2,'JOHN',2547,SYSDATE-140);
INSERT INTO EMP VALUES(1,'ALEEN',2548,SYSDATE-160);
COMMIT;

CREATE INDEX emp_idx_1 ON EMP
  (empno,ename
  );

CREATE Bitmap INDEX emp_idx_2 ON EMP
  (
    empno,ename
  )
INVISIBLE;
```

Note one of the indexes is invisible and both indexes are of different type. You can change this anytime as below:

```
ALTER INDEX emp_idx_1 INVISIBLE;
ALTER INDEX emp_idx_2 VISIBLE;
```

You can even create **unique** and **non-unique** index on the same set of columns.

```
CREATE UNIQUE INDEX E_U_IDX ON EMP(ENAME);
ALTER INDEX E_U_IDX INVISIBLE;
CREATE INDEX E_NU_IDX ON EMP(ENAME);
```

Feature 14.1: Inter-rows W Pattern matching for stock price fluctuation using "MATCH_RECOGNISE" clause

Here we will explore which stocks have undergone price fluctuation as per "W" pattern using oracle 12c "MATCH_RECOGNISE" clause

With the advent of "BIG data" the requirement for creation and capture of more and more data is increasing day by day.
Along with extra data, the business requirement of finding different patterns in data is growing rapidly.
A pattern is a repetitive series of events. Pattern can be found everywhere and in the current scenario of big data it is very much a business requirement to analyse a specific dataset and find a particular pattern.

Examples of real life scenarios can be
  ➢ Finding stock price ups and down pattern
  ➢ Finding malicious activity by some intruder
  ➢ Crime pattern
  ➢ Predict specific phone call pattern
  ➢ Fraud detection

Prior to 12c in order to detect a specific pattern it was a very difficult and complex job using analytic function, recursive queries using connect by and "WITH" clause and many self joins.
However in **oracle 12c** this pattern matching is simplified using "MATCH_RECOGNIZE" clause. This clause lets you take a dataset then group it into sets of data and order it based on timestamp and then look for a specific patterns in those partitions/groups.
Oracle Regular expression match pattern within the same record/row and 12c MATCH_RECOGNIZE match patterns across rows boundaries. So **regular expression** works for **intra-rows** whereas 12c **match_recognize** works for **inter-rows**.

Example:
Let us take one example of stock price fluctuation and let us find the stocks which have undergone price fluctuation as per pattern "**W**". This means stock is at certain value then price dips a couple of time and then price goes up and then price goes down and up again forming W shape pattern of price for a specific stock within certain period of time.

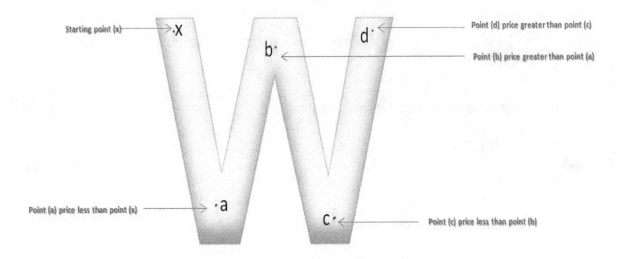

```
create table stock_price(name varchar2(30),price number(10,3),times date);

insert into stock_price values('xyz',80,to_date('15-01-2016 07:10:10','dd-mm-yyyy hh24:mi:ss'));
insert into stock_price values('xyz',90,to_date('15-01-2016 08:10:10','dd-mm-yyyy hh24:mi:ss'));
insert into stock_price values('xyz',25,to_date('15-01-2016 10:10:10','dd-mm-yyyy hh24:mi:ss'));
insert into stock_price values('xyz',24,to_date('15-01-2016 14:10:10','dd-mm-yyyy hh24:mi:ss'));
insert into stock_price values('xyz',27,to_date('16-01-2016 10:10:10','dd-mm-yyyy hh24:mi:ss'));
insert into stock_price values('xyz',26,to_date('16-01-2016 16:10:10','dd-mm-yyyy hh24:mi:ss'));
insert into stock_price values('xyz',28,to_date('16-01-2016 18:10:10','dd-mm-yyyy hh24:mi:ss'));
insert into stock_price values('xyz',20,to_date('17-01-2016 10:10:10','dd-mm-yyyy hh24:mi:ss'));

insert into stock_price values('xyz1',250,to_date('19-01-2016 10:10:10','dd-mm-yyyy hh24:mi:ss'));
insert into stock_price values('xyz1',240,to_date('20-01-2016 14:10:10','dd-mm-yyyy hh24:mi:ss'));
insert into stock_price values('xyz1',270,to_date('21-01-2016 10:10:10','dd-mm-yyyy hh24:mi:ss'));
insert into stock_price values('xyz1',260,to_date('22-01-2016 16:10:10','dd-mm-yyyy hh24:mi:ss'));
insert into stock_price values('xyz1',280,to_date('23-01-2016 18:10:10','dd-mm-yyyy hh24:mi:ss'));
insert into stock_price values('xyz1',200,to_date('24-01-2016 10:10:10','dd-mm-yyyy hh24:mi:ss'));

insert into stock_price values('xyz2',200,to_date('19-01-2016 10:10:10','dd-mm-yyyy hh24:mi:ss'));
insert into stock_price values('xyz2',300,to_date('20-01-2016 14:10:10','dd-mm-yyyy hh24:mi:ss'));
insert into stock_price values('xyz3',400,to_date('21-01-2016 10:10:10','dd-mm-yyyy hh24:mi:ss'));
insert into stock_price values('xyz3',500,to_date('22-01-2016 16:10:10','dd-mm-yyyy hh24:mi:ss'));
insert into stock_price values('xyz3',350,to_date('23-01-2016 18:10:10','dd-mm-yyyy hh24:mi:ss'));
insert into stock_price values('xyz3',500,to_date('24-01-2016 10:10:10','dd-mm-yyyy hh24:mi:ss'));

alter session set nls_date_format='dd-mm-yyyy hh24:mi:ss';
```

Note for **stock xyz** the values 90 to 28 as shown inside an oval shape form the W shape pattern.

Similarly, for **stock xyz1** values 250 to 280 as shown inside an oval shape form the W shape pattern.

But **stock xyz3** does not form the W shape pattern.

In order to find records with W shape pattern here is the solution using MATCH_RECOGNISE clause in 12c,

```
                    select * from stock_price
```

The MEASURES clause defines the columns to `match_recognize( partition by name order by times`

be shown as output produced for each match → `measures FIRST(a.times) as first_dips_time,` ← Shows the 1st dips time in W shape(point a)

`                    LAST(d.times) as last_ups_time,` — Shows the final ups time in W shape(point d)

Starting price at point x → `x.price as first_max_price,`

Price in point a in W shape → `a.price as first_dips_price,`

Price in point b in W shape → `b.price as second_ups_price,`

Price in point c in W shape → `c.price as third_dips_price,`

Price in point d in W shape → `d.price as fourth_ups_price`

`                    ONE ROW PER MATCH` ← This shows one non duplicate row for the pattern

`                    PATTERN (x a+ b+ c+ d+)` ← This shows the pattern : x is starting point and hence no +

A, b, c, d are name of points in W shape and has + means fluctuation here

`                    DEFINE --x as (price=max(price)),`

Here you define the rule for
each point in the shape, Since x is →
starting point there is no rule for this

```
                        a as (price<PREV(price)),
                        b as (price>PREV(price)),
                        c as (price<PREV(price)),
                        d as (price>PREV(price) AND d.times-FIRST(a.times)<=7));
```

↑

This shows the pattern only within 7 days span

In the pattern clause supported operators and their meaning:

- ➤ * for 0 or more iterations
- ➤ + for 1 or more iterations
- ➤ ? for 0 or 1 iterations
- ➤ { n } for exactly n iterations (n > 0)
- ➤ { n, } for n or more iterations (n >= 0)
- ➤ { n, m } for between n and m (inclusive) iterations (0 <= n <= m, 0 < m)
- ➤ { , m } for between 0 and m (inclusive) iterations (m > 0)

The **output** will be as below (the W shape picture is given to explain the output)

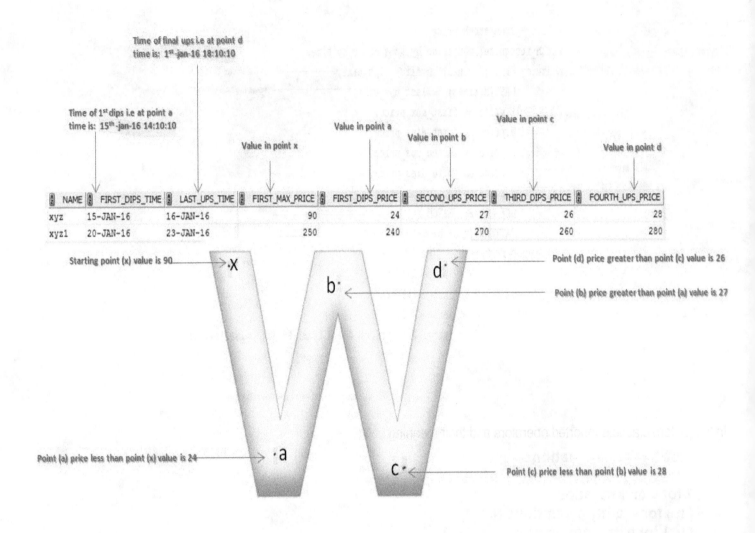

Time of final ups i.e at point d
time is: 1ˢᵗ-jan-16 18:10:10

Time of 1ˢᵗ dips i.e at point a
time is: 15ᵗʰ-jan-16 14:10:10

Value in point x

Value in point a

Value in point b

Value in point c

Value in point d

NAME	FIRST_DIPS_TIME	LAST_UPS_TIME	FIRST_MAX_PRICE	FIRST_DIPS_PRICE	SECOND_UPS_PRICE	THIRD_DIPS_PRICE	FOURTH_UPS_PRICE
xyz	15-JAN-16	16-JAN-16	90	24	27	26	28
xyz1	20-JAN-16	23-JAN-16	250	240	270	260	280

Starting point (x) value is 90

Point (d) price greater than point (c) value is 26

Point (b) price greater than point (a) value is 27

Point (a) price less than point (x) value is 24

Point (c) price less than point (b) value is 28

Similarly you can find V shape pattern or any other pattern from the dataset using this new feature in 12c. This seems to be a fairly nice feature as you can refactor the dataset across the rows and display in any format and find any pattern with ease.

Feature 14.2: Find Inter-rows Specific colour Pattern for Animal colour registration

Here we will find all the animals which are registered consecutively as Red, blue, green and yellow prior to oracle 12c and in 12c.

Prior to 12c detecting a specific pattern was a very difficult and complex job using analytic function, recursive queries using connect by, inline views etc.

Example:
Let us take one example of animal registration where each animal has a specific colour.
The requirement is to find the pattern where Red, Blue, Green and Yellow colour appear consecutively based on animal registration id.
Here you can see the specific colour combination appears 2 times.

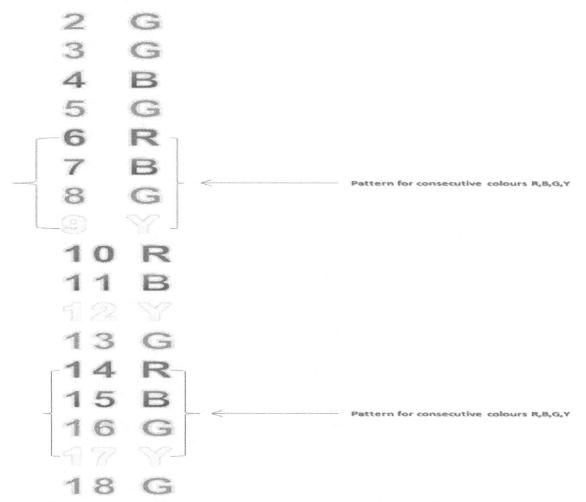

2	G
3	G
4	B
5	G
6	R
7	B
8	G
9	Y
10	R
11	B
12	Y
13	G
14	R
15	B
16	G
17	Y
18	G

Pattern for consecutive colours R,B,G,Y

Pattern for consecutive colours R,B,G,Y

In order to get the pattern prior to 12 you need to write the following analytic query which will give the animal_ids for which the pattern is found.

Prior to 12c Solution:

```
create table anilmal_colour(animal_id number,colour varchar2(10));
insert into anilmal_colour values(1,'Red');
insert into anilmal_colour values(2,'Yellow');
insert into anilmal_colour values(3,'Green');
insert into anilmal_colour values(4,'Red');
insert into anilmal_colour values(5,'Green');
insert into anilmal_colour values(6,'Yellow');
insert into anilmal_colour values(7,'Red');
insert into anilmal_colour values(8,'Red');
insert into anilmal_colour values(9,'Red');
insert into anilmal_colour values(10,'Red');
insert into anilmal_colour values(11,'Blue');
insert into anilmal_colour values(12,'Green');
insert into anilmal_colour values(13,'Yellow');
commit;
```

The analytic query to get the pattern:

```
SELECT *
FROM anilmal_colour
WHERE (animal_id) IN
  (SELECT regexp_substr(animal_ids_str,'[^,]+',1,level)  ⟵───── This will display all the ids in unpivoted rows
  FROM
    (SELECT animal_id
      ||','
      ||next_animal_id
      ||','
      ||second_next_animal_id
      ||','
      ||third_next_animal_id animal_ids_str
    FROM
      (SELECT d.*,
        lead(colour) over(order by animal_id) next_colour,
        lead(animal_id) over(order by animal_id) next_animal_id,
        lead(colour,2) over(order by animal_id) second_next_colour,
        lead(animal_id,2) over(order by animal_id) second_next_animal_id,
        lead(colour,3) over(order by animal_id) third_next_colour,
        lead(animal_id,3) over(order by animal_id) third_next_animal_id
      FROM anilmal_colour d
      )
    WHERE colour          ='Red'
    AND next_colour        ='Blue'
    AND second_next_colour='Green'
    AND third_next_colour ='Yellow'
    )
  CONNECT BY regexp_substr(animal_ids_str,'[^,]+',1,level) IS NOT NULL
  );
```

This give next colour, for this case Blue →

This give 2nd next colur, for this case Green →

This give 3rd next colour, for this case Yellow →

This will display all the ids in unpivoted rows

The output will be:

ANIMAL_ID	COLOUR
10	Red
11	Blue
12	Green
13	Yellow

Oracle 12c solution using match_recognize:

Using Oracle match_recognize it is fairly simple.

30

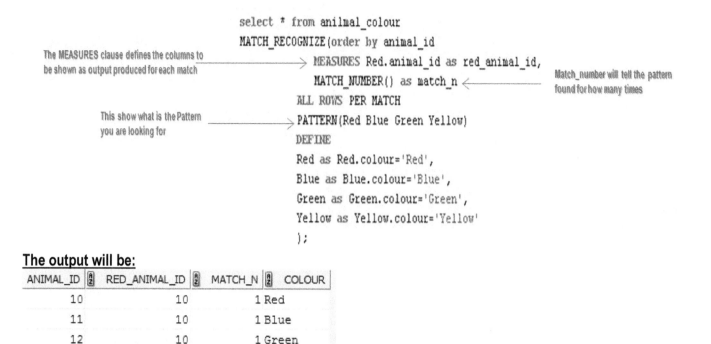

The MEASURES clause defines the columns to be shown as output produced for each match

This show what is the Pattern you are looking for

Match_number will tell the pattern found for how many times

```
select * from anilmal_colour
MATCH_RECOGNIZE(order by animal_id
        MEASURES Red.animal_id as red_animal_id,
        MATCH_NUMBER() as match_n
ALL ROWS PER MATCH
PATTERN(Red Blue Green Yellow)
DEFINE
Red as Red.colour='Red',
Blue as Blue.colour='Blue',
Green as Green.colour='Green',
Yellow as Yellow.colour='Yellow'
);
```

The output will be:

ANIMAL_ID	RED_ANIMAL_ID	MATCH_N	COLOUR
10	10	1	Red
11	10	1	Blue
12	10	1	Green
13	10	1	Yellow

Feature 14.3: Find Inter-rows Specific pattern for consecutive same flag for 3 times

Here we will discuss how to find the rows with same flags for 3 consecutive times in 12c and prior to 12c.

Example:

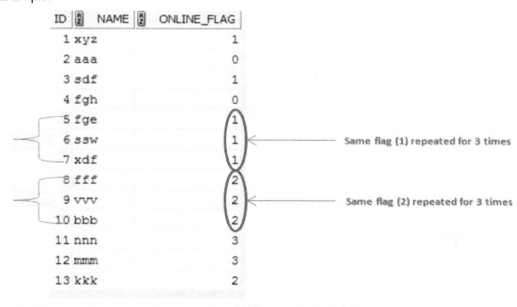

ID	NAME	ONLINE_FLAG
1	xyz	1
2	aaa	0
3	sdf	1
4	fgh	0
5	fge	1
6	ssw	1
7	xdf	1
8	fff	2
9	vvv	2
10	bbb	2
11	nnn	3
12	mmm	3
13	kkk	2

Same flag (1) repeated for 3 times

Same flag (2) repeated for 3 times

So for this case the pattern is seen in ids [5,6,7] and ids [8,9,10]
Prior to 12c you need to use an analytic function to achieve this
Solution prior to 12c:

```
create table dc_customer(id number,name varchar2(30),online_flag number);
insert into dc_customer values(1,'xyz',1);
insert into dc_customer values(2,'aaa',0);
insert into dc_customer values(3,'sdf',1);
insert into dc_customer values(4,'fgh',0);
insert into dc_customer values(5,'fge',1);
insert into dc_customer values(6,'ssw',1);
insert into dc_customer values(7,'xdf',1);
insert into dc_customer values(8,'fff',2);
insert into dc_customer values(9,'vvv',2);
insert into dc_customer values(10,'bbb',2);
insert into dc_customer values(11,'nnn',3);
insert into dc_customer values(12,'mmm',3);
insert into dc_customer values(13,'kkk',2);
```

The analytic query to get the pattern:

```
SELECT *
FROM dc_customer
WHERE (id) IN
  (SELECT regexp_substr(cust_ids_str,'[^,]+',1,level)      ← This will display all the ids in unpivoted rows
  FROM
    (SELECT id
    ||','
    ||next_id
    ||','
    ||second_next_id as cust_ids_str
      FROM
    (SELECT d.*,
      lead(online_flag) over(order by id) next_online_flag,        ← This give next consecutive flag
      lead(id) over(order by id) next_id,
      lead(online_flag,2) over(order by id) second_next_online_flag, ← This give 2nd next consecutive flag
      lead(id,2) over(order by id) second_next_id
    FROM dc_customer d
    )
  where online_flag=next_online_flag                       ←
  and online_flag=second_next_online_flag                  ← This make sure 3 consecutive flags are same
  )
  CONNECT BY regexp_substr(cust_ids_str,'[^,]+',1,level) IS NOT NULL
);
```

The output will be:

32

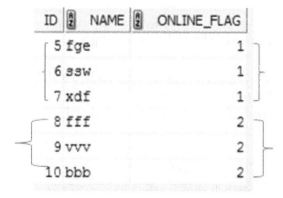

Oracle 12c solution using match_recognize:

Using Oracle match_recognize it is fairly simple.

```
select * from dc_customer
           MATCH_RECOGNIZE
           (
           order by id
           MEASURES same_flag.online_flag as same_flag_val,
           MATCH_NUMBER() as match_n
           ALL ROWS PER MATCH
           PATTERN(same_flag{3})  ←———————— This show pattern is 3 consecutive flag are same
           DEFINE
           same_flag as same_flag.online_flag=first(same_flag.online_flag)
           );
```

The output will be:

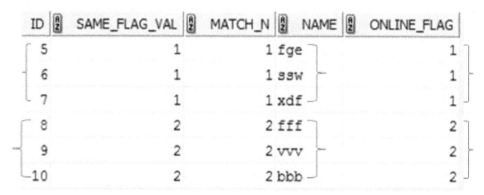

Now if you want to find the pattern where 4 consecutive flags are the same then just use this:

```
PATTERN(same_flag{4})  ←——————This show pattern is 4 consecutive flag are same
```

Now for our example four consecutive IDs with the same flag are not present and hence if you run the query based on same_flag {4} the query won't return any output.

Here we will discuss different ways of pinning an object (or part of the object) in memory for better performance.

When you run a query multiple times in the same session the response time reduces because blocks are cached and, as per LRU algorithm, are subsequently aged out of the cache block. Caching means pinning the data.
So when you talk about "Caching object" it means you PIN the object in memory. So here we will discuss Oracle 12c new feature "IN-MEMORY" column store

In-memory Column-store (IM-COLUMN) is a mechanism (introduced in Oracle 12c) by which performance critical subset of a table is placed in the "in-memory column store" which is the new section of the SGA in Oracle 12c. This "in-memory area" can be configured using "INMEMORY_SIZE" initialization parameter. You can store whole table, set of columns, specific group of columns, materialized view, table partition etc. in the IM-COLUMN store.
In-memory storage not only helps accessing data in memory, it helps reporting, business intelligence and high performance analytical queries run faster by its internal algorithm to keep the data in columnar format instead of traditional row format.

Example how to configure:

```
ALTER SYSTEM SET SGA_TARGET=4G SCOPE=SPFILE;
ALTER SYSTEM SET INMEMORY_SIZE=2G SCOPE=SPFILE;   <———— Enabling the IN-MEMORY
SHUTDOWN IMMEDIATE;
STARTUP;


                                                  Disabling the IN-MEMORY SYSTEM level
ALTER SYSTEM SET INMEMORY_SIZE=0;   <—————————
ALTER SESSION SET INMEMORY_SIZE=0;  <—————————
SHUTDOWN IMMEDIATE;                                Disabling the IN-MEMORY SESSION level
STARTUP;
```

Example how to use IM-COLUMN store (IMDB in short):

```
CREATE TABLE t1
   (
     id NUMBER,
      a  NUMBER,
      b  NUMBER,
      c  NUMBER,
      d  NUMBER,
      e  NUMBER,
      f  NUMBER
   )
   INMEMORY;   <——————— This clause keep the table in IMDB
```

In-memory (IM) setting for this table can be changed as below:

```
ALTER TABLE t1 NO INMEMORY;                    Table out of IMDB

ALTER TABLE t1 INMEMORY;                        Full Table in IMDB

ALTER TABLE t1  NO INMEMORY(b,c,d);            Only b, c, d columns are out of IMDB

ALTER TABLE t1  INMEMORY(b,c);                 b, c, columns are again in IMDB
```

For materialized view the command is:

```
CREATE MATERIALIZED VIEW t1_mview INMEMORY
AS SELECT * FROM t1;
```

As per Oracle documentation:

IM column store is good in the following scenarios:

- Large scans using "=", "<", ">" and "IN" filters, IN-MEMORY join use bloom filter.
- When it selects few columns from a table with large number of columns.
- Join small tables to large tables.
- In-memory aggregation.

IM column store is not good in the following scenarios:

- Complex predicates in the join
- Join returning large set of columns and large number of rows.
- Join large table to large table.

Chapter 2: ORACLE PL/SQL NEW FEATURE

Feature 1: WITH Clause improvement in 12c

Here we will discuss how inlining of PL/SQL function/procedure is done in 12c without using Pragma inline.

Inlining is the process by which oracle internally replaces the stored program code in the calling program, this in-turn removes context switching and so results in better performance.

Prior to 12c inlining was possible only for a view, to inline a function/procedure you needed to use PRAGMA **INLINE** as below in the function/procedure call from other subprogram.
```
PRAGMA INLINE (normal_f, 'YES ');
```

However **in 12c** you can INLINE function/procedure using "**WITH**" clause. You can have faster running procedure or function if they are defined and declared inside "WITH" clause of SQL statement.
In order to use "WITH" clause in **PL/SQL** you need to use dynamic sql.

Let us take one example to demonstrate how it works:
(**Note:** PL/SQL function using "WITH clause" does not work in some version of **SQLDEVELOPER**, so you must use sql*plus in case it does not work in your SQLDEVELOPER version for trying out all the examples given here.
)

```
SQL> create table test1(id number);

Table created.

SQL> insert into test1 values(1);

1 row created.

SQL> insert into test1 values(2);

1 row created.

SQL> insert into test1 values(3);

1 row created.

SQL> commit;

Commit complete.

SQL> WITH FUNCTION with_fun(v_id IN NUMBER) RETURN NUMBER IS BEGIN RETURN v_id;
  2    END;
  3    SELECT with_fun(id) FROM test1 WHERE rownum=1
  4  /

WITH_FUN(ID)
------------
           1
```

In order to call the WITH clause from subquery you must use WITH_PLSQL hint as below:

```
SQL> select /*+ WITH_PLSQL */ * from
  2  (
  3  WITH FUNCTION with_fun(v_id IN NUMBER) RETURN NUMBER IS BEGIN RETURN v_id;
  4  END;
  5  SELECT with_fun(id) FROM test1 WHERE rownum=1
  6  )
  7  /

WITH_FUN(ID)
------------
           1
```

If you do not use "WITH_PLSQL" hint then SQL SELECT statement will fail with error:

```
SQL> select * from
  2  (
  3  WITH FUNCTION with_fun(v_id IN NUMBER) RETURN NUMBER IS BEGIN RETURN v_id;
  4  END;
  5  SELECT with_fun(id) FROM test1 WHERE rownum=1
  6  )
  7  /
```

```
ORA-32034: unsupported use of WITH clause
```

To use procedure and function together use the below (I have formatted the output in SQLDEVELOPER for rest of the examples):

Set serveroutput on

```
WITH PROCEDURE with_proc(v_id IN NUMBER) IS
BEGIN DBMS_OUTPUT.put_line('v_id is:'
  || v_id);
END;
FUNCTION with_fun(
    v_id IN NUMBER)
  RETURN NUMBER
IS
BEGIN
  with_proc(v_id);
  RETURN v_id;
END;
SELECT with_fun(id) FROM test1 WHERE rownum = 1
/
```

This will return
```
WITH_FUN(ID)
-----------------
1
v_id is:1
```

In PL/SQL if you want to use a procedure or function using a "WITH" clause, you must use dynamic sql.
Normal functions/procedures are stored in the server, the procedure/function using "WITH" clause is inline which means the SQL engine does not need to do context switching and hence performs faster, greatly improving performance.

Here is a PL/SQL example:

Set serveroutput on

```
DECLARE
  v_sql VARCHAR2(2000);
  v_cur SYS_REFCURSOR;
  v_val NUMBER;
BEGIN
  v_sql := 'WITH
FUNCTION with_fun(v_id IN NUMBER) RETURN NUMBER IS
BEGIN
RETURN v_id;
END;
SELECT with_fun(id)
FROM   testl
WHERE  rownum = 1';
  OPEN v_cur FOR v_sql;
  FETCH v_cur INTO v_val;
  DBMS_OUTPUT.put_line('v_val is:' || v_val);
  CLOSE v_cur;
END;
/
```

You can compare the performance yourself by calling stored function and inline function using "WITH" clause in a **PL/SQL** block and loop it for larger set of records.

You can use the WITH FUNCTION/PROCEDURE in update statement using "WITH_PLSQL" operator. This operator is used like an oracle hints by embedding in UPDATE statement. If you do not use the operator then the statement will fail:

```
UPDATE testl a
SET a.id =
(
WITH FUNCTION with_fun(p_id IN NUMBER) RETURN NUMBER IS
BEGIN RETURN p_id;
END;
SELECT with_fun(a.id) FROM dual
);
```

Output:

```
ORA-32034: unsupported use of WITH clause
```

Here is the solution to update using "WITH_PLSQL" operator:

```
UPDATE /*+ WITH_PLSQL */ test1 a
SET a.id =
(
WITH FUNCTION with_fun(p_id IN NUMBER) RETURN NUMBER IS
BEGIN RETURN p_id;
END;
SELECT with_fun(a.id) FROM dual
);
```

This will update table "test1" successfully. Actually this "WITH_PLSQL" operator will let you define the function/procedure as temporary object using "WITH" clause.

Note: PL/SQL function using WITH clause does not work in some version of SQLDEVELOPER, so you must use sql*plus in case it does not work in your SQLDEVELOPER version.
You can further improve the performance of inline PL/SQL function using WITH clause by including **PRAGMA UDF** in the declaration section of inline functions.

```
WITH FUNCTION with_fun(v_id IN NUMBER) RETURN NUMBER IS
PRAGMA UDF;
BEGIN RETURN v_id;
END;
SELECT with_fun(id) FROM test1 WHERE rownum=1;
```

Use of **PRAGMA UDF** you will see in subsequent feature 3

So in oracle 12c you need not store "**one time use only**" kind of functions in data dictionary but use them as local object directly by means of "WITH" clause.
Another **note:** "WITH" clause cannot be used directly in PL/SQL but can be used in PL/SQL using Native dynamic sql as shown.

Feature 2: Reference a package constant from SQL SELECT

Here we will discuss how to call a package constant from SQL select, it is not possible to directly call this prior to 12c.

Prior to 12c you could not refer a package constant from SQL SELECT.

However in 12c you can call a package constant from select statement.
e.g.
```
CREATE OR REPLACE PACKAGE test_pkg
    IS
        v_app_scheme_type CONSTANT number  :=1;
        v_rej_scheme_type CONSTANT number := 2;
    END;
    /
```

If you try to call the package constant from SQL select it fails:
```
SELECT test_pkg.v_app_scheme_type FROM customer_tab WHERE id=111;
```

It fails **prior to 12c with error PLS-221** v_scheme_type is not a function

To resolve this **prior to oracle 12c** there are two options:

Approach1:

→Alter the package to add a function

→Create the package body in which the new function returns v_app_scheme_type.

→Then you can call the package constant from sql select via a function call.

Approach 2

Call the select from PL/SQL block.

However **in 12c** it is very simple, just call the package constant as below.

```
WITH FUNCTION v_app_scheme_type RETURN NUMBER IS BEGIN
RETURN test_pkg.v_app_scheme_type;
END;
SELECT v_app_scheme_type FROM customer_tab WHERE id=111;
```

The "WITH CLAUSE" feature is very useful SQL enhancement in oracle 12c.

Feature 3: PRAGMA UDF to improve function call from SQL

Here we will discuss compiler directive UDF to remove context switch between SQL and PL/SQL for function. This Pragma UDF is used to rearrange/inline a code for better performance.

SQL and PL/SQL has different memory representation and hence when a PL/SQL function is called from a select statement there are context switches between SQL and PL/SQL engines.

To resolve this Oracle 12c has introduced inlining using "WITH FUNCTION" clause which will invoke the function instantly in the SELECT statement with no context switching.

Also to resolve the context switching Oracle 12c has introduced "PRAGMA UDF". This is a compiler directive which states that the function is a "user defined function" and this function is used primarily in SQL select statement.

So the "WITH FUNCTION" and "PRAGMA UDF" similarity is that both are inlining the function and reduce the context switches between SQL and PL/SQL engines.

Difference between the two is:

"WITH FUNCTION" defines the PL/SQL subprogram **inside** the SQL statement.

"PRAGMA UDF"   defines the PL/SQL subprogram **outside** the SQL statement.

Converting a normal function to PRAGMA UDF function is the better approach because:

1. Using Pragma UDF you can make the code procedural and hence maintenance is easy and
   Less chance of making mistake
2. Get the advantage of inlining function which reduces context switches.
3. Moving from existing normal function to UDF function is fairly straightforward as against
   "**WITH FUNCTION**" clause which requires massive code changes where there is a function call in your application.

However if you are not worried about point **1 and 3** mentioned here then it is advisable to use "WITH FUNCTION" rather than "PRAGMA UDF" as I have seen "WITH FUNCTION" outperform "PRAGMA UDF" many times. In any case you must try all the approaches before finalizing your choice.

Both "**WITH FUNCTION**" and "**PRAGMA UDF**" method perform better than conventional function as long as these functions are called from SQL select statement. However if the "PRAGMA UDF" function is called from PL/SQL using direct call e.g. v1:=fun_pragma_udf (para1) then "PRAGMA UDF" method will drastically reduce the performance compared to a normal function. This is because Oracle "PRAGMA UDF" definition itself states the usage of this clause is beneficial only if the function is called from SQL SELECT.

Here is one example how to use "PRAGMA UDF"

```
CREATE OR REPLACE
  FUNCTION func_upper_udf(
     v_empid NUMBER)
    RETURN VARCHAR2
  IS
    PRAGMA UDF;<——————————— This is the only change in the function
    v_ename VARCHAR2(30);
  BEGIN
    SELECT upper(ename) INTO v_ename FROM emp WHERE empid=v_empid;
    RETURN v_ename;
  END func_upper_udf;
  /
```

In order to call the UDF function it is advisable to call it from SQL SELECT **as below** to get best performance:

```
DECLARE
  v_sql VARCHAR2(32767);
  v_cur SYS_REFCURSOR;
TYPE t_tab_name
IS
  TABLE OF VARCHAR2(30) INDEX BY BINARY_INTEGER;
  v_tab_name t_tab_name;
BEGIN
  v_sql :='SELECT func_upper_udf(empid) from emp';
  OPEN v_cur FOR v_sql;
  FETCH v_cur BULK COLLECT INTO v_tab_name;
  CLOSE v_cur;
END;
/
```

However if you call it as below the UDF function **performs slowly in fact it runs slightly slower than normal function without UDF PRAGMA**

```
DECLARE
  v_ename VARCHAR2(30);
BEGIN
  FOR i IN
   (SELECT empid FROM emp
   )
  LOOP
    v_ename :=func_upper_udf(i.empno);
  END LOOP;
END;
/
```

To get best benefit of "WITH clause function" and "function with PRAGMA UDF", you must call those functions from SQL SELECT statement.

So here are the suggestions in the order of best performance
→1ˢᵗ Try with SQL select if you can achieve the same functionality as the function.
→2ⁿᵈ Try a **function** using **Result cache or user**
→3ʳᵈ Try with SQL select and "WITH FUNCTION" clause if you are not worried about maintenance Cost.
→4ᵗʰ Use "PRAGMA UDF" in your function
→5ᵗʰ Use conventional function

Note: This is just a suggestion, however before choosing any approach you must try all the options mentioned and accordingly take a call for your situations.

Restriction of PRAGMA UDF
When IN or OUT parameter of a function is of data type "DATE" then UDF performs slowly
When the IN parameter data type (varchar2) has got any default value then UDF performs slowly.

Feature 4: Sensitive data masking using REDACTION

Here we will discuss how to anonymize or mask sensitive data in 12c and prior to 12c in order to protect data from unwanted exposure.

Prior to 12c you could anonymize or mask sensitive data using FGAC/VPD or by using procedural approach of masking data by implementing some rules and then de-masking the data using the reverse rule. However in 12c using data redaction policy you can on the fly mask any sensitive data of a table. Oracle 12c Redaction is the extension to the FGAC/VPD used for masking in 10g.
Oracle Data Masking is available only with Enterprise Edition and it requires licensing of Advanced Security.

Prior to 12c (in 10g) solution:

Connect to sys:
```
GRANT EXECUTE ON dbms_rls TO U1;
```

Connect to U1:

```
create table dc_cust(ID number,bank_acc number(10),bank_name varchar2(30));

insert into dc_cust values(1,1234567898,'ABC bank');
insert into dc_cust values(2,1234566897,'ABC bank');
insert into dc_cust values(3,1234565896,'ABC bank');
insert into dc_cust values(4,1234564895,'ABC bank');
insert into dc_cust values(5,1234563894,'ABC bank');
insert into dc_cust values(6,1234562893,'ABC bank');
commit;


CREATE OR REPLACE FUNCTION dc_bank_f (v_owner IN VARCHAR2, v_tab IN VARCHAR2)
RETURN VARCHAR2 AS
  v_rule VARCHAR2 (200);
BEGIN
  v_rule := 'id >0';
  RETURN (v_rule);
END dc_bank_f;
/
```

v_rule := 'id >0';   This function set the rule as to which records the masking will be implemented
RETURN (v_rule);   So if you give ID between 10 and 30 then the masking of bank_acc will happen only
                     for those ID, Other ID will have full bank_acc displayed.

```
BEGIN
  DBMS_RLS.ADD_POLICY (object_schema      => 'U1',
                       object_name        => 'dc_cust',
                       policy_name        => 'mask_bank_acc',
                       function_schema    => 'U1',
                       policy_function    => 'dc_bank_f',
                       sec_relevant_cols  => 'bank_acc',
                       sec_relevant_cols_opt => DBMS_RLS.ALL_ROWS);
END;
/
```

object_name → Name of the table on which you will mask the sensitive columns

sec_relevant_cols → This will state list of columns (separated by commas) will be masked

sec_relevant_cols_opt → This allows to display all the row of the table But mask only the value as per function dc_bank_f

Now when you run

```
select id,bank_acc,bank_name from dc_cust;
```

The bank_acc value will be masked:

ID	BANK_ACC	BANK_NAME
1		ABC bank
2		ABC bank
3		ABC bank
4		ABC bank
5		ABC bank
6		ABC bank

In order to de-mask or remove the masking use this:

```
BEGIN
  DBMS_RLS.DROP_POLICY (object_schema  => 'U1',
                        object_name    => 'dc_cust',
                        policy_name    => 'mask_bank_acc');
END;
/
```

43

Oracle 12c (and also backported to 11.2.0.4) has introduced DBMS_REDACT package to define redaction policy for masking sensitive data of tables and this provides greater level of control and protection of sensitive data and it is much easier to implement as shown below:

Data redaction is part of advanced security option. **It does not change the actual data, it just hides the sensitive data from the unauthorized user.**

12c solution for full masking:

Connect to sys:

```
GRANT EXECUTE ON sys.dbms_redact TO U1;
```

Connect to U1:

```
BEGIN
  DBMS_REDACT.add_policy(
    object_schema => 'U1',
    object_name   => 'dc_cust',
    column_name   => 'bank_acc',        <———  This will state list of columns
                                              (separated by commas) will be masked
    policy_name   => 'redact_mask_bank_acc',
    function_type => DBMS_REDACT.full,  <———  Function_type state what kind of masking will take
    expression    => '1=1'                    Place like if it is full or some part of the string of the
  );                                          sensitive column will be masked
END;
/                   ↑
        This means redaction will always take place
```

Expression=>'1=1' means masking will happen for all users. However if you want to implement the masking for a set of users or not to mask for a set of users then use the following expression instead of "1=1"

```
expression      => 'SYS_CONTEXT(''USERENV'',''SESSION_USER'') != ''U2'''
```

This means redaction/masking will not take place for schema "U2" and hence from schema u2 if you run "**select * from U1.dc_cust;**" you will see actually original value (not the masked value of bank_acc.

Now when you run from user U1

```
select id,bank_acc,bank_name from dc_cust;
```

You will get bank_acc value masked to 0:

ID	BANK_ACC	BANK_NAME
1	0	ABC bank
2	0	ABC bank
3	0	ABC bank
4	0	ABC bank
5	0	ABC bank
6	0	ABC bank

12c solution for using substituted value:

If you want to display the substituted value instead of original value you can do that by adding additional parameter [FUNCTION_PARAMETRS] in add_policy or alter_policy function as shown below:

```
BEGIN
  DBMS_REDACT.alter_policy (
    object_schema      => 'U1',
    object_name        => 'dc_cust',
    policy_name        => 'redact_mask_bank_acc',
    action             => DBMS_REDACT.modify_column,
    column_name        => 'bank_acc',
    function_type      => DBMS_REDACT.partial,    <------ Function_type state what kind of masking will take
    function_parameters => '9,1,6'                        Place like if it is partial then some part of the string of the
  );                                                      sensitive column will be masked as per function_parameters
END;
/
```

This state how the redaction will be masked.
1st parameter 9: value to be masked to
2nd parameter 1: start point of the string to be masked
3rd parameter 6: end point of the string to be masked

So here 1st to 6th character of bank_acc column value will be replaced by 9

If the data type of **column** (Intended to be masked) is other than **number** then function_parameters will accordingly use different type of values/arguments.

Now when you run

```
select id,bank_acc,bank_name from dc_cust;
```

You will get bank_acc 1 to 6th character values masked to 9:

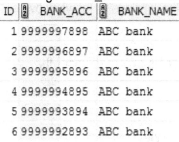

ID	BANK_ACC	BANK_NAME
1	9999997898	ABC bank
2	9999996897	ABC bank
3	9999995896	ABC bank
4	9999994895	ABC bank
5	9999993894	ABC bank
6	9999992893	ABC bank

From SQLDEVELOPER you can do this by selecting Add Redaction policy and subsequently adding a policy function.

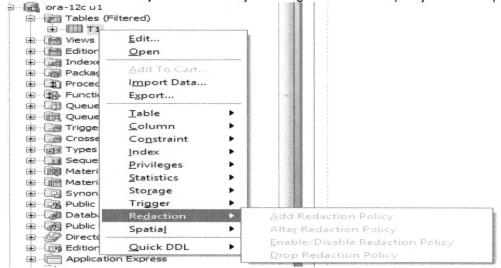

In order to de-mask (disable redaction) or remove the masking use this in oracle 12c:

```
BEGIN
  DBMS_REDACT.drop_policy (
    object_schema => 'U1',
    object_name   => 'dc_cust',
    policy_name   => 'redact_mask_bank_acc'
  );
END;
/
```

Note: Redaction policy is not applicable for Sys user because SYS has "EXEMPT REDACTION POLICY" and hence if you run the following from SYS user:

```
SELECT id,bank_acc,bank_name FROM u1.dc_cust;
```

It will show bank_acc without any kind of masking.

Feature 5: Define view to act like invoker right programmer unit

Invoker right function behaves like invoker right even if it is called from view which is definer right, intriguing? Here we will discuss how it is done in 12c using BEQUEATH clause in a view. Prior to 12c an invoker right function behaves like definer right when it is called from view (View is definer right).

Prior to 12c when a view is executing/calling a function then the function is executed under the privilege of the view owner as per the rule below:

When an "**invoker right code**" is called by "**definer right code**" then the "**invoker right code**" is executed under the authority of "**definer right code**".

So if you have a "**invoker right function**" and it is called by a view (default of view is definer right)
Then the function will act as if it is definer right and will give result as per the owner of definer (**view owner**).

Often the expectation is that whoever invokes the function the result should be in accordance to that because the function is invoker right code.

Let us take one example:

Prior to 12c this is how it works:

46

```
connect U1

CREATE TABLE app
(
    app_id      INTEGER,
    dept_id     INTEGER,
    app_name        VARCHAR2 (50)
);

    INSERT INTO app VALUES (1, 10, 'CG');
    INSERT INTO app VALUES (2, 20, 'LLK');
    INSERT INTO app VALUES (3, 30, 'SUB');
    COMMIT;

CREATE OR REPLACE
  FUNCTION app_cnt(
      dept_id_in IN NUMBER)
    RETURN NUMBER AUTHID CURRENT_USER
  IS
    v_cnt NUMBER;
  BEGIN
    SELECT COUNT (*) INTO v_cnt FROM app WHERE dept_id = dept_id_in;
    RETURN v_cnt;
  END app_cnt;
  /
CREATE OR REPLACE VIEW app_cnts_view
AS
    SELECT dept_id,
           app_cnt (dept_id)
           count_of_app
     FROM app;
/


GRANT SELECT ON app_cnts_view TO U2
/
```

Now connect to U2 and create same "APP" table with different data as below:

```
connect U2

CREATE TABLE app
(
    app_id      INTEGER,
    dept_id     INTEGER,
    app_name        VARCHAR2 (50)
);

    INSERT INTO app VALUES (4, 10, 'CG_L1');
    INSERT INTO app VALUES (5, 10, 'CG_L2');
    INSERT INTO app VALUES (6, 10, 'CG_L3');
    INSERT INTO app VALUES (7, 40, 'LLK1');
    INSERT INTO app VALUES (8, 50, 'SUB2');
    COMMIT;
```

Two approaches to execute the function

Approach 1(Via view)
Now if you run as below from the view (**which will internally execute the function**):

47

```
connect U2
select * from U1.app_cnts_view;
```
You will get following result:

This come view → DEPT_ID COUNT_OF_APP ← This come from function
Based on U1.app   call based on u1.app

DEPT_ID	COUNT_OF_APP
10	1
20	1
30	1

This result COUNT_OF_APP is derived based on the function app_cnt executed from user u1 even if the function is invoker right code and expected to invoke as per the authority of user U2.

Approach 2 (via direct function call)

However if you run the function directly by giving require execute privilege and grant to U2 it will give the result as below, note COUNT_OF_APP is derived based on U2.app as expected because function is invoker right code.
```
connect U2
select dept_id,U1.app_cnt(dept_id) count_of_app from U1.app;
```

This come view → DEPT_ID COUNT_OF_APP ← This come from function
Based on U1.app   call based on u2.app

DEPT_ID	COUNT_OF_APP
10	3
20	0
30	0

So the result set COUNT_OF_APP of calling the function from "a view" and "executing independently from a sql" are entirely different. However expectation is that, the invoker right function should return exactly same way from both the **approaches** and the result should be as given in **approach 2.**

Prior to 12c it was not possible to get the result look like **approach 2** when the invoker right function is called from a view which can **only** be definer right.

In 12c, oracle has introduced **BEQUEATH** clause for view so it will not convert an invoker right function to definer right. In other words by using this clause, VIEW will keep the function in its purest form and intention.
So solution in 12c
Just add the BEQUEATH clause in the view definition as below:

```
connect U1

CREATE OR REPLACE VIEW app_cnts_view
BEQUEATH CURRENT_USER
AS
    SELECT dept_id,
           app_cnt (dept_id)
           count_of_app
      FROM app;
/


GRANT SELECT ON app_cnts_view TO U2
/
```

```
connect U2
select * from U1.app_cnts_view;
```

This come view ———→ DEPT_ID | COUNT_OF_APP ←——— This come from function
Based on U1.app

DEPT_ID	COUNT_OF_APP
10	3
20	0
30	0

call based on U2.app

So in 12c you can see the function **app_cnt** is executed as invoker right (**here U2 is the invoker**) even if it is called by a VIEW because you can see under user U2 you have **3** applications in **dept_id=10** and **0** application count in department **20, 30**.

Note: The view "u1.app_cnts_view" itself is not invoker right code even if you use

BEQUEATH CURRENT_USER

It is evident by the result because it returns the dept_id from **U1 schema** which is the owner of the view not from user **U2** who invokes the view.

Feature 6: Restructuring error stack

Here we will demonstrate how to display the contents of error stack to find the root cause of an issue in 12c.

Prior to Oracle 12c you can print the error details as below:
Dbms_output.put_line (DBMS_UTILITY.FORMAT_ERROR_STACK)

However the output of the error is much unstructured and to determine the root cause of an issue is tedious.

In 12c Oracle has introduced UTL_CALL_STACK package to display the content of the error stack in proper format. It has 3 API ERROR_DEPTH, ERROR_MSG, and ERROR_NUMBER.

The below API using **utl_call_stack** need to be created one time in your database and can be called by any code in your oracle PL/SQL application:

```
CREATE OR REPLACE
PROCEDURE show_error_stack
AS
  v_depth NUMBER;
BEGIN
  v_depth := UTL_CALL_STACK.error_depth;
  DBMS_OUTPUT.PUT_LINE('Depth      Err code     Error message');
  DBMS_OUTPUT.PUT_LINE('----------   -----------  --------------------');
  FOR i IN 1 .. v_depth
  LOOP
    DBMS_OUTPUT.PUT_LINE( RPAD(i, 12) || RPAD('ORA-' ||
    LPAD(UTL_CALL_STACK.error_number(i), 5, '0'), 12) ||
    UTL_CALL_STACK.error_msg(i) );
  END LOOP;
END show_error_stack;
/
```

49

Now you can call this API in any of your PL/SQL code

```
SET serveroutput ON
DECLARE
  v_name VARCHAR2(30);
BEGIN
  SELECT employee_name INTO v_name FROM emp WHERE sal=1250;
EXCEPTION
WHEN OTHERS THEN
  show_error_stack;
END;
/
```

The output:
```
anonymous block completed
Depth        Error code    error msg
-----------  -----------   ---------
1            ORA-01422     exact fetch returns more than requested number of rows
```

Feature 7: Restructuring backtrace

Here we will demonstrate how to display the line number and program details to find where is the root cause.

Prior to Oracle 12c you can print the line number when an exception is raised using:
Dbms_output.put_line (DBMS_UTILITY. FORMAT_ERROR_BACKTRACE)

However the output of the backtrace information regarding the block and the line number of the error propagated is much unstructured.

In 12c Oracle has introduced UTL_CALL_STACK package to display the content of the backtrace in proper format. It has 3 API BACKTRACE_DEPTH, BACKTRACE_LINE, and BACKTRACE_UNIT.

The below api using utl_call_stack need to be created one time in your database and can be called by any code in your oracle PL/SQL application to backtrace the line number and responsible subprogram:

50

```
CREATE OR REPLACE
PROCEDURE show_backtrace_stack
AS
  v_depth NUMBER;
BEGIN
  v_depth := UTL_CALL_STACK.backtrace_depth;
  DBMS_OUTPUT.PUT_LINE('Depth       Line no     Unit');
  DBMS_OUTPUT.PUT_LINE('-----------  -----------  --------------------');
  FOR i IN 1 .. v_depth
  LOOP
    DBMS_OUTPUT.put_line( RPAD(i, 12) ||
    RPAD(TO_CHAR(UTL_CALL_STACK.backtrace_line(i),'99'), 12) ||
    UTL_CALL_STACK.backtrace_unit(i) );
  END LOOP;
END show_backtrace_stack;
/
```

Now you can call this API in **any of your PL/SQL code**

```
SET serveroutput ON
DECLARE
  v_name VARCHAR2(30);
BEGIN
  SELECT employee_name INTO v_name FROM emp WHERE sal=1250;
EXCEPTION
WHEN OTHERS THEN
  show_backtrace_stack;
END;
/
```

OUTPUT:
```
anonymous block completed
Depth        Line no      Unit
-----------  -----------  ---------
1                4
```

Note: UNIT value is null as it is anonymous block

Procedure execution:

```
CREATE OR REPLACE PROCEDURE backtrace_test_proc
IS
  v_name VARCHAR2(30);
BEGIN
  SELECT employee_name INTO v_name FROM emp WHERE sal=1250;
EXCEPTION
WHEN OTHERS THEN
  show_backtrace_stack;
END backtrace_test_proc;
/
SET serveroutput ON
exec backtrace_test_proc
```

```
anonymous block completed
Depth        Line no       Unit
-----------  -----------   ----------
1            5             ANONYMOUS.BACKTRACE_TEST_PROC
```

Feature 8: PL/SQL only data type support in "native dynamic SQL", "SELECT call" And "as a bind variable"

Here we will discuss the usage of PL/SQL only datatype like BOOLEAN, associative array in **"SQL select"** ,**"TABLE operator"** and **"native dynamic sql"** from PL/SQL in 12c.

Prior to Oracle 12c you could not bind **PL/SQL only specific datatype** (e.g. Boolean, associative array which do not exist in SQL but exists in PL/SQL) in dynamic SQL and also they cannot be used in "SQL SELECT" statements.
However, 12c improves the usability of PL/SQL and hence "SQL unsupported data type" can be used in native dynamic SQL and SQL select statement in PL/SQL anonymous block.

Simple example to demonstrate how it works in 12c and fails in 11g
Common step:

Create the function containing Boolean data type
```
CREATE TABLE t2 AS
SELECT * FROM all_objects WHERE rownum<20;


CREATE OR REPLACE FUNCTION f_object_name (
    object_id_in    IN t2.object_id%TYPE,
    v_upper_req            IN BOOLEAN)
    RETURN t2.object_name%TYPE
IS
    v_return    t2.object_name%TYPE;
BEGIN
    SELECT object_name
      INTO v_return
      FROM t2
     WHERE object_id = object_id_in;

    RETURN CASE WHEN v_upper_req THEN UPPER (v_return) ELSE LOWER(v_return) END;
END;
/
```

This function is created fine both in 11g and 12c database. This function returns the object name in upper case when Boolean value (v_upper_req) is TRUE, otherwise object name is returned in lower case.

Call from anonymous block using function call:

Call this from anonymous block using function call

```
set serveroutput on
declare
v_obj_name t2.object_name%TYPE;
v_upper_req BOOLEAN :=TRUE;
Begin
v_obj_name :=f_object_name(365,v_upper_req);
dbms_output.put_line(v_obj_name);
end;
/
```

→This works fine both in 11g and 12c as this is the basic functionality

Call from anonymous block using SQL select:

When the following code is called from SQL "**select**" statement inside an anonymous block it **fails in 11g** and run **fine in 12c**:

```
SET serveroutput ON
DECLARE
  v_upper_req BOOLEAN :=TRUE;
BEGIN
  FOR i IN
  (SELECT f_object_name(object_id,v_upper_req) obj_name
  FROM t2
  WHERE object_id=365
  )
  LOOP
    dbms_output.put_line(i.obj_name);
  END LOOP;
END;
/
```

→Prior to 12c it fails with error wrong number of argument <u>because "v_upper_req" is Boolean</u>
→In Oracle 12c onward it is successful as Boolean which a PL/SQL only data type is
   Supported now in "SELECT call in PL/SQL".

Dynamic SQL using bind variable:

```
SET serveroutput ON
DECLARE
  v_upper_req BOOLEAN :=TRUE;
BEGIN
  EXECUTE immediate 'BEGIN dbms_output.put_line
  (f_object_name(365,:bind)); END;' USING v_upper_req;
END;
/
```

53

→Prior to 12c it fails with error

```
PLS-00457: expressions have to be of SQL types
```

→In Oracle 12c onward it is successful.

Associative array call in SELECT and as TABLE operator

Prior to 12c you could not use associative array in "SQL select" and as "Table operator" or as bind variable, you can only use this in PL/SQL expression as below:

Example

```
CREATE OR REPLACE PACKAGE pkg
AS
    TYPE t1
    IS TABLE OF VARCHAR2 (30)
        INDEX BY BINARY_INTEGER;

    PROCEDURE show_name (
        names    IN t1);
END pkg;
/


CREATE OR REPLACE PACKAGE BODY pkg
AS
    PROCEDURE show_name (
        names    IN t1)
    IS
    BEGIN
        FOR i IN 1 .. names.COUNT LOOP
            DBMS_OUTPUT.put_line ( 'The name is:'||names(i));
        END LOOP;
    END;
END pkg;
/
```

Run the following both in 11g and 12c to test the effect of using bind variable for associative array in dynamic sql:

```
SET serveroutput ON
DECLARE
  v_names pkg.t1;
BEGIN
  v_names(1) :='scott';
  v_names(2) :='Stephen';
  v_names(3) :='Asim';
  EXECUTE immediate 'begin pkg.show_name(:names); end;' USING v_names;
END;
/
```

Error in 11g:

54

```
PLS-00457: expressions have to be of SQL types
```
The error is displayed because associative array (v_names is PL/SQL only data type) is not supported as bind variable prior to 12c

Output in 12c:
```
anonymous block completed
name is:scott
name is:Stephen
name is:Asim
```

Run the following both in 11g and 12c to test the effect of TABLE operator:

```
SET serveroutput ON
DECLARE
  v_names pkg.tl;
BEGIN
  v_names(1) :='scott';
  v_names(2) :='Stephen';
  v_names(3) :='Asim';
  FOR j IN
  (SELECT * FROM TABLE(v_names)
  )
  LOOP
    dbms_output.put_line(j.column_value);
  END LOOP;
END;
/
```

Error in 11g:
```
PL/SQL: ORA-22905: cannot access rows from a non-nested table item
```
The error is displayed because you could not use associative array in TABLE operator prior to 12c

Output in 12c:
```
anonymous block completed
scott
Stephen
Asim
```

Solution prior to 12c:
The only way you can call this in 11g, is to avoid bind variable/table operator as shown below:

```
set serveroutput on
DECLARE
    v_names    pkg.tl;
BEGIN
    v_names (1) := 'scott';
    v_names (2) := 'Stephen';
    v_names (3) := 'Asim';
pkg.show_name(v_names);
END;
/
```

Other way to make this works prior to 12c is to change the package to use nested table instead of associative array.

However in 12c as shown, PL/SQL developer has the flexibility to execute the function/package in many different ways even if they use associative array in the application.

Note: BOOLEAN, ASSOCIATIVE ARRAY **are only available** in PL/SQL but **not available** in SQL.
However other data type like VARCHAR2, CHAR are present both in SQL and PL/SQL.
Both CHAR and VARCHAR2 are used to store string values. The only difference between the 2 is: CHAR is fixed length variable and hence if you declared a variable as **CHAR (10)** and try to store value "ASIM" then remaining 6 character will be stored as 6 spaces whereas **VARCHAR2 (10)** is varying length **variable/data type** and hence if you store "ASIM" remaining 6 character will not be padded with space and hence these 6 bytes will be available for others to use.

Feature 9: White listing and accessible by clause

This is another new feature of Oracle 12c.
Here we will explore how to prevent a user from executing a sensitive sub-program even if he has execute privilege. This is one more layer of security which ensure that the sensitive program is accessible by authorized set of package/procedure/functions.

Using "**grant** execute on package/procedure" you can grant privilege to execute certain package or procedure to a specific user. PL/SQL cannot prevent a user from executing a subprogram to which he has been granted execute authority.
However using **white listing** by means of "accessible by" clause Oracle 12c enhances security by restricting the right to execute a specific subprogram to the users/procedures/package/functions which are in the white list.
E.g. to demonstrate the usage of accessible by clause

```
CREATE OR REPLACE
PACKAGE white_pkg
IS
PROCEDURE p1;
END;
/


CREATE OR REPLACE
PACKAGE protected_pkg ACCESSIBLE BY(white_pkg)
IS
PROCEDURE protected_p1;
PROCEDURE protected_p2;
END;
/
```

56

Note **protected_pkg** can only be accessed by **white_pkg** from a session as "**white_pkg**" is in the accessible by clause. You can give any number of users/package/procedure in the accessible by clause and separate them by comma e.g. (white_pkg1, white_pkg2, white_pkg3, procudre1).

Now let us create the package body for both the above packages.

```
CREATE OR REPLACE PACKAGE body white_pkg
IS
    PROCEDURE p1 is
    BEGIN
    protected_pkg.protected_p1;
    protected_pkg.protected_p2;
    END;
END;
/


CREATE OR REPLACE PACKAGE BODY protected_pkg
IS
    PROCEDURE protected_p1 IS
    BEGIN
    dbms_output.put_line('inside protected_p1');
    END;

    PROCEDURE protected_p2 IS
    BEGIN
    dbms_output.put_line('inside protected_p2');
    END;
END;
/
```

Now you can execute the protected_pkg as below (via white_pkg):

```
begin
white_pkg.p1;
end;
/
```

This will give output as below:
```
inside protected_p1
inside protected_p2
```

However if you try to execute the package <u>independently</u> it will fail as below:

```
set serveroutput on
begin
protected_pkg.protected_p1;
protected_pkg.protected_p2;
end;
/
PLS-00904: insufficient privilege to
access object PROTECTED_PKG
```

Also try to call the protected_pkg <u>procedure from other program</u>, it will fail as below:

```
CREATE OR REPLACE PROCEDURE test_proc
IS
BEGIN
    protected_pkg.protected_p1;
END;
/
```

```
PLS-00904: insufficient privilege to
access object PROTECTED_PKG
```

So now you can see using white listing "protected_pkg" can be referred/called only by the program mentioned in ACCESSIBLE BY clause of "protected_pkg" package.

Feature 10: Invoker right code with Result_cache

Here we will see how **result_cache** work for invoker right code.

Oracle 11g has introduced function result cache however you cannot combine RESULT_CACHE for invoker right code. In **Oracle 12c** this restriction is lifted.
Here is one example

```
CREATE OR REPLACE
  FUNCTION f_object_name(
      object_id_in IN t2.object_id%TYPE)
    RETURN t2.object_name%TYPE AUTHID CURRENT_USER RESULT_CACHE
  IS
    v_return t2.object_name%TYPE;
  BEGIN
    SELECT object_name INTO v_return FROM t2 WHERE object_id = object_id_in;
    RETURN v_return;
  END;
  /
```

So in Oracle 11g if you run this it will fail with error:

```
PLS-00999: implementation restriction (may be temporary) RESULT_CACHE is disallowed on subprograms in Invoker-Rights modules
```

However the above is successful in Oracle 12c because oracle will pass the current_user as hidden parameter along with the argument value passed to the result cache function. So you will get performance benefit of result cache if the **same current user** executes the same function with same argument value. However normal result cache with definer right code gets the benefit of results cached by function calls done by **any users.**

Feature 11: Returning implicit statement result set

Here we will demonstrate how to return the resultset implicitly to client applications.

Prior to 12c Oracle returns the result-set from stored subprogram to client (like sql*plus, Java, oci or any other client application) by defining explicitly REF CURSOR as OUT parameter.
And in the call to the stored procedure from sql*plus, JAVA or any other client application you need to

Fetch from the REF CURSOR, store the result-set and loop through each result-set to display the value in client application.

So here are the steps **prior to 12c**

```
CREATE OR REPLACE
PROCEDURE show_object_name(
    object_type_in IN all_objects.object_type%TYPE,
    v_cur OUT SYS_REFCURSOR)
IS
BEGIN
  OPEN v_cur FOR SELECT object_name FROM all_objects
  WHERE object_type=object_type_in AND rownum<10;
END;
/
```

Prior to 12c you can return the **result set explicitly** to the client application as below:

```
SET serveroutput ON
DECLARE
  v_cur SYS_REFCURSOR;          <----------- Step 1
type obj_tl
IS
  TABLE OF VARCHAR2(30) INDEX BY binary_integer;
  v_obj_tl obj_tl;             <--------- Step 2
BEGIN
  show_object_name('SYNONYM',v_cur);
  FETCH v_cur bulk collect INTO v_obj_tl;<---- Step 3
  FOR i IN 1..v_obj_tl.count <--------- Step 4
  LOOP
     dbms_output.put_line(v_obj_tl(i)) <------- Step 5
  END LOOP;
END;
/
```

However in 12c you can return the **result set implicitly** to the client application as below:

```
CREATE OR REPLACE
PROCEDURE show_object_name(
    object_type_in IN all_objects.object_type%TYPE )
IS
 v_cur SYS_REFCURSOR;
BEGIN
  OPEN v_cur FOR SELECT object_name FROM all_objects
  WHERE object_type=object_type_in AND rownum<10;
  DBMS_SQL.return_result (v_cur);
END;
/
EXEC show_object_name('SYNONYM');
```

So you can see in 12c it is so simple to return the result set **implicitly** to client application.

Feature 12: Improvement in conditional compilation

Here we will show the new predefined inquiry directives which are introduced in 12c

$$PLSQL_UNIT_OWNER Owner of the PL/SQL unit
$$PLSQL_UNIT_TYPE: Type of PL/SQL unit like procedure/function/package etc.

You can display the value as below:

Dbms_output.put_line('Owner of the unit:'||$$PLSQL_UNIT||' ←——————— Introduced in 10g
                              is:'||$$PLSQL_UNIT_OWNER||'
        And the type of the unit is:'||$$PLSQL_UNIT_TYPE ↑
              );

                                        Introduced in 12c

Feature 13: Granting a Role to PL/SQL subprogram instead of USER

Here we will discuss how to provide role to a subprogram instead of granting role to a schema and avoid a big security threat.

By default subprograms are created based on definer right.
Execute privilege on the subprogram must be granted to the invoking schema by the definer schema in order to call the subprogram from a different schema
From the invoking schema you can execute the subprogram even if you do not have access to underlying structure (i.e. you cannot **select/insert/delete** from the table mentioned in the subprogram from SQL but can access through subprogram). This is fine in **definer right** subprogram as you do not expose the underlying structure to the invoking schema.

However when you use **invoker right** subprogram which executes under the authority of invoker you need to provide grant (**on the underlying objects**) to the calling user via role/explicit privilege and thus exposing the owner's table completely to the invoking schema. So before 12c each and every subprogram which is called from another schema has same privilege on the owner's tables and hence you expose the schema owner's tables completely to the invoking user.

However in 12c each subprogram when called from another schema could have different privileges on the owner table.

Just to simplify in oracle 12c you can have **function** func1, func2 and **procedure** proc1, proc2 in **schema u1** and each subprogram referring to a table (say t1) from same schema **u1**
But in the calling schema (say **schema u2**) each and every subprogram will have different privilege on the table from **schema u1**. So for example
Func1 may have select privilege on u1.t1
Func2 may have insert privilege on u1.t1
Proc1 may have update privilege on u1.t1
Proc2 may have delete privilege on u1.t1
And schema u2 has no privilege at all and hence schema owner u2 cannot do any operation independently (like select, insert, update or delete from sqlplus). [**Prior to 12c all the privileges percolates to calling user u2 always which could cause security issue as the privileges are exposed completely to the user.**]

60

Let us take one example how the code based access control works.

```
ALTER session SET "_ORACLE_SCRIPT"=true;
DROP USER u1 CASCADE;
DROP USER u2 CASCADE;
CREATE USER u1 IDENTIFIED BY u1 QUOTA UNLIMITED ON USERS;
CREATE USER u2 IDENTIFIED BY u2 QUOTA UNLIMITED ON USERS;

GRANT CREATE SESSION,CREATE TABLE, CREATE PROCEDURE TO u1,u2;
CONNECT TO u1

CREATE TABLE t1
    (a NUMBER,b VARCHAR2(30)
    );

  INSERT INTO t1 VALUES
    (1,'test'
    );
  COMMIT;
CREATE OR REPLACE
PROCEDURE proc_invoker AUTHID CURRENT_USER
IS
  x VARCHAR2(30);
BEGIN
  SELECT b INTO x FROM u1.t1;
  dbms_output.put_line('the value of x is:'||x);
END proc_invoker;
/

GRANT EXECUTE ON proc_invoker TO u2;

CONNECT TO u2

SELECT * FROM u1.t1;

SET serveroutput ON
EXEC u1.proc_invoker;
```

Both the "SELECT statement" and "procedure proc_invoker execution" will fail with error
`ORA-00942: TABLE OR VIEW does NOT exist`

To resolve this prior to 12c here is the step:
```
CONNECT TO SYS

CREATE role r1;
GRANT r1 TO u1,u2;
GRANT SELECT ON u1.t1 TO r1;

CONNECT TO u2
SELECT * FROM u1.t1;
SET serveroutput ON
EXEC u1.proc_invoker;
```

Now both the "SELECT statement" and "procedure execution" will succeed.
But the problem is now u1.t1 is exposed completely to user u2
In 12c we can have code based access control so that u1.t1 is not exposed to user but can have different privileges on different subprogram as per your requirement.

So 12c solution is:

```
CONNECT TO SYS
REVOKE r1 FROM u2;
GRANT r1 TO PROCEDURE u1.proc_invoker;
```

If you want to grant UPDATE privilege to the procedure u1.proc_invoker then run this:

```
[
CONNECT TO SYS
CREATE role r2;
GRANT r2 TO u1;
GRANT UPDATE ON u1.t1 TO r2;
GRANT r2 TO PROCEDURE u1.proc_invoker;
]
```

Similarly sys user can give some other privilege to other subprogram of your schema. (**Note you do not provide any privilege to the invoking user, you only provide privilege to the program unit**)

So now if you run

```
CONNECT TO u2
SELECT * FROM u1.t1;
```

It will fail as expected because **schema u2** does not have the privilege.
But the procedure will run fine as the role has been granted to the procedure only.

```
CONNECT TO u2
SET serveroutput ON
EXEC u1.proc_invoker;
```

Chapter 3: ORACLE ADMINISTRATION NEW FEATURES

Feature 1: Adaptive query optimization and online stats gathering

Here we will discuss improvement in accuracy of execution plan and enhancement in online statistics gathering in 12c.

Adaptive query optimization is the **new feature** in 12c which helps the optimizer to improve the accuracy of an execution plan.

The purpose of oracle optimizer is to determine the best execution plan for a SQL statement. It makes the decision based on the statistics available and the optimizer used and execution features available in the Oracle release.
If no statistics are available then using dynamic sampling it generates some sample statistics and decides the execution plan.
Please note fixed object statistics (pre 12c approach) do not always give sufficient information to find the most accurate and best execution plan.

In Oracle 12c Oracle has introduced **adaptive query optimization**. This consist of **2 aspects**:

Adaptive plan: This enables the optimizer to delay the final execution plan until the execution of the query is completed. This is done by making adjustments at run-time using dynamic sampling and cardinality feedback. As the query runs, information is collected from and passed between each part of the execution plan, allowing the adaptive plan to switch between the HASH and NESTED LOOP join methods as required.

Adaptive statistics: This provides additional information to improve subsequent execution of the query.

Online stats gathering:
In oracle 12c dynamic sampling has been enhanced to have online stats gathering (known as dynamic statistics). The dynamic stats improve the existing statistics by getting more accurate cardinality estimates for tables, Join clause, group clause etc. Initialization parameter OPTIMIZER_DYNAMIC_SAMPLING value "11" enables the optimizer to automatically collect dynamic statistics.
For example, because online stats gathering results are instantly available to the optimizer, we have seen substantial performance improvement when using CTAS (**Create table as select * from**) and IAS (**Insert into ...Select * from**).

Note: If optimizer is not using correct execution plan the query which is expected to finish in few minutes might take few hours due to incorrect cardinality estimates, absence of statistics or out of date statistics.

Feature 2: Faster online table column addition & length of an object name

Here we will demonstrate that addition of default nullable column in pre-12c, locks the system for a certain duration and generates huge undo and redo, however in 12c this issue is resolved.

In Oracle 11g if you need to add a default column which can be nullable it takes a significant amount of time. However if the default column is not nullable then it is instantaneous.
So the addition of a nullable default column performance issue is addressed in Oracle 12c

Here is one example

Run this in Oracle 11g:
```
CREATE TABLE t2 AS
SELECT * FROM all_objects;
```

Add a default column which is NOT NULL,
```
ALTER TABLE t2 ADD (c5 CHAR(100) DEFAULT 'yes' NOT NULL)
```
This takes 0.4 sec.

Add a default column which is NULLABLE,
```
ALTER TABLE t2 ADD (c6 CHAR(100) DEFAULT 'yes')
```
This takes 15-25 sec and for this duration it will lock the entire table. Also this operation generates large amount of undo and redo.

However, when you run exactly same operations in **12c** both will take less than 0.4 sec and there is no locking.

To see the size growth of the table you can do as below in 11g and 12c:
Step 1:

```
ANALYZE TABLE T2 compute statistics;

SELECT AVG_ROW_LEN*NUM_ROWS/1024/1024
  ||' MB' size_of_table
FROM all_tables
WHERE owner   ='SCHEMA_NAME'
AND table_name='T2';
```

Step 2:
```
ALTER TABLE t2 ADD (c6 CHAR(100) DEFAULT 'yes')
```
Step 3:
```
ANALYZE TABLE T2 compute statistics;
SELECT AVG_ROW_LEN*NUM_ROWS/1024/1024
  ||' MB' size_of_table
FROM all_tables
WHERE owner   ='SCHEMA_NAME'
AND table_name='T2';
```
You can see there is significant growth in table size in oracle 11g, However in oracle 12c the growth is nominal.

Object/identifier length: From Oracle 12.2 onward the length of a literal can be max 128 bytes. Earlier length of a database object name can be maximum of 30 bytes. So now you can create a table or package whose name can contain more than 30 characters and up to 128 bytes.

Feature 3: DDL LOGGING and ONLINE DDL

Here we will discuss how oracle write the DDL history in a dedicated log file and also understand how ONLINE DDL are performed.

Oracle 11g has introduced parameter **ENABLE_DDL_LOGGING** which will write DDL into alert log file
The alert log file is very large making it difficult to find the DDL versions.

However in Oracle 12c all the DDL is written into a dedicated log file located in "ADR Home"/log/DDL.

ADR Home can be found using below query:
```
SELECT name, value FROM v$diag_info WHERE name='ADR Home';
```

In order to log the DDL activity you need to enable the parameter
```
ALTER session SET enable_ddl_logging=true;
```

The DDL log records creation, alteration and drop of packages/procedures/function/Table/Trigger.
This is very useful when you need to know when a different version of a DDL statement was executed and by whom.

So now it is possible to reverse engineer the database as the log captures all versions and times of DDL execution.

ONLINE DDL:
ONLINE DDL signifies you can perform DML operations while doing alteration (DDL) of objects. In Oracle 12c you can perform few DDL operations ONLINE.
```
DROP INDEX EMP_IDX ONLINE FORCE;
ALTER TABLE EMP DROP CONSTRAINT CONS_NM ONLINE;
ALTER INDEX EMP_IDX VISIBLE;
ALTER INDEX EMP_IDX INVISIBLE;
ALTER INDEX EMP_IDX1 UNUSABLE ONLINE;
ALTER TABLE EMPLOYEES SET UNUSED (HIREDATE) ONLINE;
```

In Oracle 11g you can perform only index rebuild ONLINE
```
ALTER INDEX index_name REBUILD ONLINE PARALLEL;
```
That means if index rebuild command is running for 30 minutes, it will not hold lock on the table for 30 min. During 30 min period you can do any DML activities.

Feature 4: Adding multiple new Partitions

Here we will show how addition of more than one partition at a time in oracle 12c is done.

Before Oracle 12c it was not possible to add more than one new partition at a time. So to add new partitions you had to execute "alter table add partition" command multiple times. However in Oracle 12c R1 you can add multiple partitions using 1 command as below:

```
Alter table mv_trans add partition
Partition trans_data_p4  VALUES LESS THAN (TO_DATE('17-7-2010','DD-MM-YYYY')),
Partition trans_data_p5  VALUES LESS THAN (TO_DATE('17-8-2010','DD-MM-YYYY')),
Partition trans_data_p6  VALUES LESS THAN (TO_DATE ('17-9-2010','DD-MM-YYYY'));
```

Feature 5: Global temporary table enhancement

Here we will find how to reduce redo generation for Global temporary tables in 12c.

Prior to 12c, Oracle global temporary tables generate huge redo because the undo segment is stored in regular undo tablespace.

However In 12c Oracle global temporary tables reduces redo generation substantially by <u>storing the undo segment in temporary</u> <u>tablespace</u> instead of undo tablespace and hence improve performance on creation of GTT. This is useful for reporting as report uses Global temporary table for achieving better performance.

Feature 6: Stats gathering improvement

Here we will demonstrate, in 12c how you can gather statistics of multiple objects in parallel

Oracle optimizer decides the best way of retrieving data from a database based on execution plan. The execution plan is generated based on statistics present in the database. <u>Oracle stats</u> contain <u>Object statistical</u> information like
  - ➢ number of rows,
  - ➢ number of distinct values,
  - ➢ smallest and largest value,
  - ➢ presence of NULL,
  - ➢ column histogram ,
  - ➢ clustering factor ,
  - ➢ Index tree depth etc.

These stats are important information used by the optimizer to estimate the selectivity of WHERE clause predicate and subsequently generate the best execution plan.
Prior to 12c oracle used to gather stats one table at a time. You could parallelize the stats gathering if the table was big enough.
So when you run this **prior to 12c**

```
EXEC DBMS_STATS.GATHER_SCHEMA_STATS('SCOTT');
```

It will gather stats for the whole schema but one object at a time.

12c solution:
In 12c you can gather stats of multiple tables, partitions concurrently.
Here is the setup for achieving this:

```
ALTER SYSTEM SET RESOURCE_MANAGER_PLAN='DEFAULT_MAIN';
ALTER SYSTEM SET JOB_QUEUE_PROCESSES  =4;
EXEC DBMS_STATS.SET_GLOBAL_PREFS('CONCURRENT', 'ALL');
```

Now you can gather stats concurrently for a schema

```
EXEC DBMS_STATS.GATHER_SCHEMA_STATS('SCOTT');
```

Feature 7: Fundamental of HEAT MAP

Prior to 12c Information Lifecycle Management (ILM) assistant performs archival of data from high performance storage to low cost storage.

Oracle 12c (under ILM) has introduced "heat map" and "automatic data optimization (ADO)" to improve data storage and compression.
Using heat map oracle internally either compress data or move data to low cost storage tablespace. It tracks when data is being accessed at table level and row level. Heat map provide specific information about the <u>age of data</u> based on hot, warm or cold as explained below:

Hot: It means data is accessed/modified frequently and last accessed/modified date is less than 2 days.
Warm: It means data is accessed/modified not so frequently and last accessed/modified date is greater than 5 days but less than 60 days.
Cold: It means data is accessed/modified rarely and last accessed/modified date is greater than 60 days.

Note: In one single table you can have all these three sets of data.

Implementation of heat map:
The "HEAT_MAP" initialization parameter is used to enable or disable heat map as well as Automatic Data Optimization (ADO). By default it is disabled (OFF).

```
ALTER session SET HEAT_MAP=ON;--session level
ALTER system SET HEAT_MAP =ON;--system level
```

Once enabled all the table and data will be tracked.
Heat map captures details (e.g. read, write, full scan, index lookup etc.) using dictionary view V$HEAT_MAP_SEGMENT and user views USER_HEAT_MAP_SEGMENT, USER_HEAT_MAP_SEQ_HISTOGRAM, USER_HEATMAP_TOP_OBJECTS.

Using heat map, oracle automates policy-driven data movement and compression. To do that DBA has to create multiple policies which compress the set of data (**hot**) in "OLTP" mode, **warm** data can be compressed using "compress for query" mode, and **cold** data can be compressed using "compress for archive" mode. Also DBA can create one more policy to move the **cold** data to low cost storage space.
These policies once created by DBA, are invoked automatically when age criteria for the data is satisfied.

Feature 8: Read only user can lock a system on a transaction, resolution using GRANT READ?

Here we will demonstrate how a user having read only access to a schema can lock the system and will discuss possible solution in 12c and prior to 12c.

In oracle you can give "grant select" on a table to a read only user using
"Grant select on table_name to read_only_user" and then **read_only_user** can run the below select from his read only session:
```
SELECT *
FROM    Prod.ref_data
FOR UPDATE;
```

However this statement will lock the table and prevent any DML operation by any user (not even the owner of the table i.e. prod) who has insert/update/delete privileges.

This is really serious situation. Prior to 12c there are two possible resolutions:
1. DBA need to kill the read only session to release the lock or
2. The read only user need to give commit or exit the session.

In 12c the situation can be avoided by giving "grant **read**" **instead** of "grant **select**" on the table to the read only user:
```
grant read on Prod.ref_data to read_user;
```

67

This means the read only user will not have sufficient privilege to run the SELECT FOR UPDATE statement.

Note: Prior to Oracle 11g you cannot make a table read only in a tablespace where other tables are read write. However 11g onward you can make a table read only and read write in the same tablespace using command:

```
ALTER TABLE <TABLE NAME> READ ONLY;
```

You can convert it into read write using

```
ALTER TABLE <TABLE NAME> READ WRITE;
```

Feature 9: Improvement in auditing using flashback

Here we will discuss 12c new feature to see who does the changes in a row.

Pre 12c Oracle flashback FDA can track changes to data however It does not capture who does the changes (**unless this column [updated_by] is present in the respective table**) which is very essential for auditing purpose.
In Oracle 12c FDA tracks complete audit of changes including user environment setting and store them as metadata.
In order to do that in Oracle 12c you need to run the following two commands after flashback is configured

Connect to sys as sysdba

```
GRANT EXECUTE ON DBMS_FLASHBACK_ARCHIVE TO DB;
GRANT CREATE ANY CONTEXT TO DB;
```

Now connect to user "DB" and run the flashback version query

```
SELECT versions_xid,
   DBMS_FLASHBACK_ARCHIVE.get_sys_context(versions_xid, 'USERENV','SESSION_USER')   session_user,
   DBMS_FLASHBACK_ARCHIVE.get_sys_context(versions_xid, 'USERENV','CLIENT_IDENTIFIER') client_identifier,
   versions_starttime,
   versions_endtime,
   versions_operation,
   test2.*
FROM test2 versions BETWEEN TIMESTAMP to_timestamp('2015-01-01 12:30:59','YYYY-MM-DD HH24:MI:SS') AND to_timestamp('2015-06-01 09:39:59','YYYY-MM-DD HH24:MI:SS')
WHERE versions_starttime >= to_timestamp('2015-01-01 12:30:59','YYYY-MM-DD HH24:MI:SS')
AND versions_starttime   < to_timestamp('2015-06-01 09:39:59','YYYY-MM-DD HH24:MI:SS')
and test2.id=1001
ORDER BY versions_starttime;
```

As marked in yellow you can see flashback query could provide the history of data changes and from stored USERENV could provide the corresponding session_user and client_identifier who made the changes.
So from an audit perspective you can find out id=1001 has undergone different changes and changes done from which session user and client_identifier.

Feature 10: Improvement in tracking history for security related table

Here we will demonstrate how to track changes for security sensitive tables.

Oracle 12c has introduced a feature called database hardening which simplifies the management of flashback data archive for a group of security sensitive tables. So in 12c you can have single command to enable FDA for a group of tables and address the need for strong auditing. The management of group of tables is done using below package.
`DBMS_FLASHBACK_ARCHIVE.`

Here are the steps to group all the required tables and handle flashback for the set of tables

Start a group:
Here you start a group call APPLICATION associated with flashback drive (DB_FDA).

```
BEGIN
  DBMS_FLASHBACK_ARCHIVE.register_application(
    application_name     => 'APPLICATION',
    flashback_archive_name => 'DB_FDA');
END;
/
```

Assigning table to the group

Here you assign set of tables e.g. T1, T2 and T3 to the group APPLICATION

```
BEGIN
  DBMS_FLASHBACK_ARCHIVE.add_table_to_application (
    application_name => 'APPLICATION',
    table_name       => 'T1',
    schema_name      => 'DB');

  DBMS_FLASHBACK_ARCHIVE.add_table_to_application (
    application_name => 'APPLICATION',
    table_name       => 'T2',
    schema_name      => 'DB');

  DBMS_FLASHBACK_ARCHIVE.add_table_to_application (
    application_name => 'APPLICATION',
    table_name       => 'T3',
    schema_name      => 'DB');

END;
/
```

Enable flashback for the group
```
BEGIN
  DBMS_FLASHBACK_ARCHIVE.enable_application(
    application_name => 'APPLICATION');
END;
/
```

Disable flashback for the group
```
BEGIN
  DBMS_FLASHBACK_ARCHIVE.disable_application(
    application_name => 'APPLICATION');
END;
/
```

Remove certain table from the group

69

```
BEGIN
  DBMS_FLASHBACK_ARCHIVE.remove_table_from_application(
    application_name => 'APPLICATION',
    table_name       => 'T2',
    schema_name      => 'DB');

END;
/
```

Drop the group from DB

```
BEGIN
  DBMS_FLASHBACK_ARCHIVE.drop_application(
    application_name => 'APPLICATION');
END;
/
```

Note: Prior to 12c we could create separate flashback archive drive for security sensitive tables.

Feature 11: import and export of flashback version history

Here we will discuss mechanism to import and export flashback version history.

Oracle 12c supports import of user generated history into existing FDA table. So users who have been maintaining history using some other mechanism (like trigger) can now import those history table to oracle 12c FDA as below:

Let us say you want to import "t2_hist" table located in "DB1" schema **into** "DB" schema and flashback table "t2" (T2 has its own flashback data and part of flashback drive DB_FDA).

Step 1
1st import t2_hist table to "DB" schema using normal means like data pump etc.

Step 2
Run the command
```
BEGIN
  DBMS_FLASHBACK_ARCHIVE.import_history (
    owner_name1       => 'DB',
    table_name1       => 'T2',
    temp_history_name => 'T2_HIST',
    options           => DBMS_FLASHBACK_ARCHIVE.NODELETE);
    -- Allowed values are NODELETE, NODROP, NOCOMMIT,
END;
/
```

Also Oracle 12c supports **export** of existing FDA table's history. Here oracle will automatically create default history table TEMP_HISTORY in the same schema

Let us say you want to export flashback history of "t2" table located in "DB" schema into "DB1" schema
Step 1
Run the command

70

```
BEGIN
  DBMS_FLASHBACK_ARCHIVE.create_temp_history_table(
    owner_namel => 'DB',
    table_namel => 'T2');
END;
/
```

This will create history track table with all version data in default table TEMP_HISTORY

Step 2
Import this temp_history table to DB1 schema using data pump or any other means and you can rename the table.

Feature 12: Free Flashback archive and OPTIMIZE option

This feature dealt with improvement in flashback archive.

Prior to 12c Flashback data archive was available only with enterprise edition however from 12c onward it is available with all editions.
Also in 12c you have extra parameter to create the flashback archive with compression or no compression option. No Compression option means no optimization and this is the default. However if you use "OPTIMIZE DATA" then it will allow you do compression and this is optimized for performance by means of compression.

Here is the command in 12c to create flashback archive drive:

```
CREATE FLASHBACK ARCHIVE DB_FDA
TABLESPACE DB_FDA_TBS
QUOTA 1G
RETENTION 1 YEAR
NO OPTIMIZE DATA;←————————      This is the extra clause introduced in 12c


CREATE FLASHBACK ARCHIVE DB_FDA
TABLESPACE DB_FDA_TBS
QUOTA 1G
RETENTION 1 YEAR
OPTIMIZE DATA;←————————      This is the extra clause introduced in 12c
```

Feature 13: Multitenant container database with Pluggable database option

Oracle 12c multitenant container database is based on the architecture for next generation cloud.
In this architecture there is a container database which hold many pluggable databases. All the pluggable databases share the same memory and background process of the container database.

Consider the scenario where in your organization you have a database with set of schema say HR, SALES, GIS, FIN and different group say "DEVELOPER", "TESTER", "DESIGNER" and "DBA" want to use the same framework to do certain work uninterrupted.

In order to achieve that you have to create 4 physical database which means you have to maintain 4 instances.

71

However in Oracle 12c by virtue of multitenant architecture you can create many pluggable databases which will share the same instance. Now same framework can be independently used by "DEVELOPER", "TESTER", "DESIGNER" and "DBA" By simply creating 4 pluggable databases.

Here are the setup:

Connect to **sys as sysdba** and run all the commands.

To see if 12c database has been created as CDB (container database) just run:
`SELECT cdb FROM v$database;`
This will return "YES" or "NO"

To see how many pluggable database are present
`SELECT con_id, dbid, name FROM v$pdbs;`

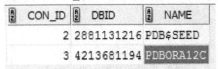

CON_ID	DBID	NAME
2	2881131216	PDB$SEED
3	4213681194	PDBORA12C

To drop a pluggable database:
`ALTER pluggable DATABASE PDBORA12C CLOSE immediate;`
`DROP pluggable DATABASE PDBORA12C including datafiles;`

Now you see how many pluggable database are present because one is dropped.
`SELECT con_id, dbid, name FROM v$pdbs;`

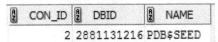

CON_ID	DBID	NAME
2	2881131216	PDB$SEED

To create a pluggable database:

`SELECT file_name FROM dba_data_files;`

FILE_NAME
C:\APP\ASIM.A\ORADATA\ORA12C\USERS01.DBF
C:\APP\ASIM.A\ORADATA\ORA12C\UNDOTBS01.DBF
C:\APP\ASIM.A\ORADATA\ORA12C\SYSTEM01.DBF
C:\APP\ASIM.A\ORADATA\ORA12C\SYSAUX01.DBF

```
CREATE pluggable DATABASE pdb_test admin USER dbaclass IDENTIFIED BY dbaclass
FILE_NAME_CONVERT=('C:\APP\ASIM.A\ORADATA\ORA12C\PDBSEED\',
'C:\APP\ASIM.A\ORADATA\ORA12C\pdb_test\');
```

`ALTER pluggable DATABASE pdb_test OPEN;`

You see how many pluggable database are present
`SELECT con_id, dbid, name FROM v$pdbs;`

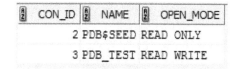

CON_ID	NAME	OPEN_MODE
2	PDB$SEED	READ ONLY
3	PDB_TEST	READ WRITE

"DEVELOPER" can use this pluggable database by running the following command:

```
ALTER session SET container=pdb_test;
```

Now he can use the common framework with set of schemas and work independently.

Similarly you can create another 3 pluggable databases for "DESIGNER", "TESTER" and "DBA"

This way each and every user can use the same framework in terms of object, schema, synonyms etc without any hindrance by other users.

This is truly a boon for database administrator.

INDEX PAGE

Query used to generate the index page:

```
SELECT upper(rpad(idx,30,'-'))
  ||page_number "Index Page"
FROM
  ( SELECT DISTINCT idx,
    listagg(page_no,',') within GROUP(
  ORDER BY page_no) over(partition BY idx) page_number
  FROM test_a
  ORDER BY 1
  )
ORDER BY 1;
```

E

F

G

H

I

L

M

N

O

P

R

S

T

U